The
Shaver Mystery Magazine
Vol 1 No 1 1947

Richard S. Shaver
Alfred Steber (Editor)

SAUCERIAN PUBLISHER
Original Sources in Ufology

ISBN: 978-1-955087-50-6

9 781955 087506

2023, Saucerian Publisher

PROLOGUE

Returning to the classics in any genre is generally a good idea. This also goes for UFO literature. Rereading a book or reviewing old documents after ten or twenty years is a rewarding experience. You will discover new data and ideas you didn't notice before. The reason, of course, is that you are, in many ways, not the same person reading the book the second or third time. Hopefully, you have advanced in knowledge, experience, and intellectual and spiritual discernment. A good starting point is to reread the UFO classics to understand the more profound mystery of what happened during that era.

This title is scarce and hard to find these days. The Shaver Mystery Magazine originally was published by the Shaver Mystery Club. This newsletter published the first printed stories on UFOs and was a major forum for debates about the occult, Forteans, and Lemurians. As Ray Palmer promoted it: "dedicated to the further study of the hidden truths as presented in the fact-fiction stories by Richard S. Shaver..."

In essence, the Shaver Mystery is a collection of stories in which Shaver claimed to have discovered proof of an evil humanity in underground caverns. Shaver portrayed an alien race that resided in Earth's caverns before escaping, leaving behind two distinct populations of offspring: the "Teros," a benevolent group of humanoids, and the "Deros," or "detrimental robots," a vile race who tormented and devoured humans. The Deros were especially brutal to women. The tales encouraged the establishment of Shaver Mystery Clubs.

The present edition is an authentic reproduction of the original Shaver Mystery Magazine printed text in shades of gray. **IMPORTANT,even though we have attempted to maintain the integrity of the original work, the present facsimile reproduction may have missing letters and blurred pages, poor pictures due to the age of the original scanned copy.** This magazine has been formatted from its original version for publication. Great, but unpretentious, this issue is an extraordinarily rare symbol of what was going on in those early years of the modern UFO phenomena.

Editor
Saucerian Publisher, 2023

The SHAVER MYSTERY MAGAZINE

Being dedicated to the further study of the hidden truths as presented in the fact-fiction stories by Richard S. Shaver, made famous in the past three years in AMAZING STORIES magazine.

Subscription Price 50c per Issue

OBTAINED ONLY

THROUGH MEMBERSHIP

THE SHAVER MYSTERY CLUB

CONTENTS

Vol. I.   1947   No. 1

EDITORIAL . . . . Page 4

LIFE ON OTHER PLANETS
  By Roger P. Graham . . . . Page 6

A PREFACE AND FOREWORD TO "MANDARK"
  By Richard S. Shaver . . . . Page 9

MANDARK (Installment one)
  By Richard S. Shaver . . . . Page 16

HEIRENS' FRIEND, GEORGE MURMAN
  By Richard S. Shaver . . . . Page 31

DO EVERTHING YOU CAN, TODAY
  By Richard S. Shaver . . . . Page 34

VOICES IN THE NIGHT
  By Richard S. Shaver . . . . Page 35

LETTERS FROM READERS
  By The Readers . . . . Page 38

Frontispiece by Malcolm Smith

THE SHAVER MYSTERY MAGAZINE

is Published by
THE SHAVER MYSTERY CLUB
2414 Lawrence Ave.
Chicago, Ill.

Richard S. Shaver, *Editor*   Chester S. Geier, *President*

EDITORIAL

THIS new magazine is dedicated to unearthing truth.

Truth is a vast thing, and few minds ever form a full concept of life, the universe, or any great part of either. Hence few minds have real contact with truth, cannot recognize it when they face it.

But the people to whom this magazine are addressed are those who have written the Editor of *Amazing Stories* about the Shaver stories, have demonstrated their ability to recognize truth however obscured. And that my efforts have failed to reveal clearly the truth I have been trying to portray, I sometimes fear.

This truth about our life and civilization is *the most important* truth, because we have to know what obstacles we face in order to overcome those obstacles.

This is the obstacle this magazine undertakes to overcome, the obstacle that is our own blindness, our inability to ferret out facts pertinent to our survival as a race.

These pertinent and necessary facts are obscured by prejudice, by religious beliefs, by teachings fostered by our pedagogical system, by the active obstructive work of those enemies we seek to expose to the eyes of their victims.

Every person I have ever talked to about the phenomena coming to be known by the name "the Shaver mystery" for want of a better, has at first denied ever having any such experiences. For fully five minutes of conversation about spooks, hob-goblins, voices in the night, dreams, etc., these people hold out—then they get a light in their eye and say: "Now that I think of it, I had a strange experience . . ." and they wind up by spending the whole evening relating incident after incident that might have been culled word for word out of a Shaver story or a ghost tales magazine. Every person has had weird or unnaturally beautiful dreams that he cannot understand, has had hair-breadth escapes from unseen forces causing a culminative catastrophe from which he could not escape, has had voices speak to him out of nowhere, and almost all of them can be got to admit these experiences by judicious extraction.

Now this magazine offers a place where all this wide-spread mine of information can be assembled so that all of us can form our own opinions on what these experiences mean to us, where the truth about these mysterious threatening things in our life can be printed and intelligently analyzed.

Each man can express his own opinion and obtain data for the growth and formation of that opinion:— are we invaded by secretive extra-terrestrials; are we victimized by monopolists of modern scientific wonders; are we suffering from a recrudescence of an old ailment (call it witchcraft, call it spirits or devils); or are we having an epidemic of crackpots telling lies?

Each of these views will be taken up exhaustively one by one, stories will be written illustrating these viewpoints, articles written about each one and about some new ones we have not yet heard about—and from all of this analysis, we hope the truth will emerge in the end.

That all this work will be colored by my own experiences in and knowledge of this field is unavoidable, and I warn you in advance to discount this if you do not believe in my words. I do not ask blind acceptance, I do ask an analytical attitude.

Religion itself endlessly corroborates the fact of the existence of these phenomena, and the fact of their existence as far back into time as the memory of man reaches. The modern attitude of complete scepticism about the existence of "supernatural" manifestations is our natural opponent, but itself has and will furnish us with endless data and unavoidably corroborative research results.

Many of these "modern" minded opponents read these stories and are vastly interested in spite of themselves—for they do explain many things otherwise completely mysterious.

These "moderns" are the intelligent products of a system of education given us by the past, complete with prejudiced, biased summations of rigidly expurgated material, complete with opinionated supervision by all too frequently sterile pedants of the most dark enlightenment. Yet they still think, they still deduce, and they cannot avoid interest in the "Shaver Mystery". For the evidence is inescapably omnipresent, obscured mainly by the blind side given our minds by the aforementioned early fathers of our pedagogy.

We have never heard of a myth in school that was not accompanied by complete and "learned" explanations of the "nature" or imaginative source of these myths. It has never occurred to the writers of these debunking books about the past that there was a greater thing in the myths than was ever put there by the mind of man as we know him. "Nature myths" is the automatic mental reaction to every "learned" persons hearing of these extremely ancient tales. "Jove's lightning" was *just any thunderbolt,* and the "savage" of the past gave thunder a personality, called it Jove or Zeus or what have you—and that was the end of speculation on these early sources of our modern "literature". Yet there is a great deal more in such fine literary efforts as the Eddas, as the Sagas, the Greek myths, behind Homer's Iliad than any savage interpretation of natural forces.

The truth is Odin *had* an "eye", it *did* see everything, and his voice *meant business.* They listened, those early surface men, and it was well they did so, for they would not have lived to hand down the myths otherwise.

But the "scientific" method does not accept such a statement by me; it must have *more.* That is why this magazine: to furnish the "more" in a quantity calculated to impress even the most prejudiced product of our modern religious atheism. He believes in God, he usually admits, but that is as far as belief carries him. He is seldom a pantheist, and only laughs when you suggest his God must have had forbears, brothers and sisters, and descendants.

Never-the-less these religious by-paths are one thing we must avoid—interesting as they are, they are not the whole point of our effort. Our effort must be directed at exposing a *threat to our survival,* none the less terrible because it is an *ancient evil.* It is still a terrible detriment to our life, one side of its activity; and on the other, it is responsible for preserving our lives from this same detriment. Why the good people of the caverns must preserve the secrecy surrounding their life, I don't know, but it is so. I have deduced that it is wholly a custom they cannot shake off, any more than we can shake-off the custom of believing everything reposing between the covers of a text book.

Our civilization is throttled by a terrible enemy. George Murman is only one small type or phase of these enemy activities. George Murman was mad, many of these enemies are also mad; but they do us endless harm, and are never apprehended that we know about.

Are spiritualists all deluded? Was Heirens deluded? Is Shaver right in his pictures of cavern life? Is modern religion, when it supports modern occurrences of "miracles", also a dupe of secret actitivities by our hidden friends and enemies?

These and similar questions will all be handled in these pages, as fully and as completely scrupulously as possible.

Here every man is to give his evidence. The reader-jury is to sum up the evidence and give the verdict.

Are Charles Fort and Richard Shaver right in saying we are "fished for" by extra-terrestrials? Is Shaver telling the truth about the caverns below the surface? In a courtroom every defendant has to prove his case, every plaintiff produce his evidence.

This editor wants you to know the truth, wants you to analyze the evidence, wants you to judge for yourself.

If there is a soul, we would like to prove that. If there is not, we want to know just why people believe in their existence, what the evidence is—we want to hear about it.

We would like to avoid all blind acceptance of dogmatic assertions, and we would like to ferret out the whole truth. We can!

Is some secret group of people engineering our wars, stealing our supplies, running things from behind a screen of secrecy?

We think they are, and we *know* the only reason for such secrecy is a *very evil reason.* People who have nothing harmful to hide would not go to such extremes.

We think man as we know him is losing his racial life to a very ugly social form, an alien race lacking everything we consider essential to civilized life! We think that unless something happens to turn the tide of this unseen struggle, man will sink into a nightmare kind of existence, a fearful substitute for our present hopeful aspirations toward a sane future! We want people everywhere to know this, so that they may fight against it! We must have more definite information to base actual counter effort upon! You readers everywhere can help with this. You must, for man's sake!

We think a large and influential portion of our people are bamboozled into placid acceptance of a destroying evil, bamboozled by a complicated facade of lies that will crumple before the tiniest light of truth. We want to free those people so that they will work for our welfare, instead of accepting our destruction.

LIFE ON OTHER PLANETS

By Roger P. Graham

(Author of Numerous Scientific Stories and Articles)

WHETHER there is life on the other planets in the solar system or not has been a topic of speculation ever since the first day it was known that Earth IS a planet, and not the center of the universe. It is a topic that has been discussed in almost every phase by writers of scientifiction. In addition, there have been countless positive assertions from "psychics" that there is intelligent life on some of these planets.

In fact, there are more than twenty witnesses that swear that on October ninth, 1946, during the rain of meteors into the atmosphere, we were visited by a space ship, and that its name was the Kareeta. It was, from some observers, "a huge, batlike affair with flapping wings," and from other observers, "an invisible thing that landed in a vacant lot and took off with a loud sound of motors." Knowledge of its name and that it was actually a space ship comes from "psychics" who assert they were in actual mental contact with it or with "spirits" who were in contact with it. They assert definitely that it came from another planet.

Obviously the scientific minded cannot take the visit of the Kareeta as proven beyond dispute. But also quite obviously, they cannot deny that it might be possible that such a ship DID come.

The "huge, bat-like wings" raises an interesting line of conjecture. Suppose such a ship were built? It would need the traction of gas to rise against gravity. Suppose the extremely tenuous gas of the comet that passed near us were sufficient to enable such a ship to rise clear of the strong pull of Earth. It *is* possible if the wings were quite large in proportion to the mass of the whole ship.

If the comet had passed some other planet close enough so that its tail contacted the atmosphere of that plane, and a ship had been built in anticipation of that occurrence, the citizens could take off, using the atmosphere of the comet to rise far above the stratosphere of their own planet, come to Earth, and land. But they couldn't stay more than a few hours or the comet would have left and they would be unable to rise free of our stratosphere! So they would be in too much of a hurry to do much gallivanting around.

They might just land in some vacant lot, rush out and get a few souvenirs for evidence of their visit, and then take off again.

This line of conjecture increases the probability that such a ship actually DID land on Earth. The implication is that at least one other planet does have intelligent life on it.

What do we really know about the other planets? Quite a bit in factual data. For example, the latest astronomical data, as listed in the 29th edition of the Handbook of Chemistry and Physics, tells us that a man would weigh exactly the same on Uranus or Neptune as he does on Earth—down to the last fraction of an ounce. Gravity on Earth, Uranus, and Neptune, by some strange coincidence is 980 cm/sec. squared.

Again, Mars and Mercury have exactly the same gravities, which are four-tenths of Earth gravity. On the moon it's a little more than a sixth of Earth gravity, and on Jupiter and Saturn gravity is supposedly 2.7 and 1.2 times that on Earth, respectively. But IS it?

Take Jupiter. "Different portions of the disk as seen in the telescope rotate with different speeds, making astronomers certain that the features observed in the telescope are not those of the actual surface. The temperature of this gas 'surface' is minus 140° Centigrade. Perhaps the most satisfactory theory today is that the plane has a small solid core surrounded by extensive and very dense atmosphere. Recent observations show the presence of ammonia gas and methane in its atmosphere."

Saturn. "As in the case of Jupiter, the disk of Saturn is marked with belts . . . which astronomers believe are clouds in the atmosphere. There is ammonia gas and methane in the atmosphere."

Now, in both these planets, Jupiter and Saturn, it is entirely possible that the surface gravity of the solid planet, under the atmospheres that hide it, is no greater than Earth gravity. The planet PLUS the atmosphere has a very great mass. Jupiter is 314.5 the mass of Earth, while its specific gravity (mean density) is a little less than one fourth that of Earth.

If we suppose that there is a solid planet under the atmosphere and that its density is about that of Earth, then Jupiter, is about 59,000 miles in diameter instead of 89,229, as supposed by direct measurement. This still makes it have a terrific volume. But its gravitational attraction (7.69) for something on the surface is cut down by the counter attraction of the twenty thousand miles of atmosphere above the surface, so that actual weight at the surface would be appreciably less than if there were little atmosphere. Furthermore, there would be a buoyancy due to the density of the atmosphere, which would be very dense at the surface, so that objects such as organic beings would not be crushed to the surface, but would be buoyed up. A man weighing two hundred pounds on Earth in air would weigh only fifty pounds on Earth in gasoline because of the buoyancy of the surrounding medium. Then he would again weigh 200 if gravity were four times that of Earth.

It is POSSIBLE that WEIGHT on the surface of the major planets is not too great for the comfort of a human being in a space suit. Native life forms developing there could evolve to the mobile, animal stage and develop intelligence.

It is fairly certain that conditions are favorable to hydrocarbon evolution. The dense atmospheres, with cold stratospheres, indicate temperatures greater than freezing and less than the boiling point of water at and near the surface.

Methane and ammonia in the stratospheres indicate that the basic conditions for beginning of life, at least, are present.

Life, as we know it on earth, is evolved from simple hydro-carbons and hydroxi-carbons, starting with perhaps the alcohols living on methane and ammonia, and later developing the cell sac from byproducts. The cell sac stabilized environment for the life process, making possible much more complex development of living molecules.

Living forms are known to thrive in pressures of thousands of pounds to the square inch, and temperatures above boiling and below freezing. Life is a natural phenomenon, developing spontaneously wherever it has the right materials and a long enough time to cover all possibilities open to it.

IT IS PRACTICALLY CERTAIN THAT THERE IS LIFE ON ALL THE PLANETS THAT HAVE ANY ATMOSPHERE. Is there INTELLIGENT life on any of them other than Earth? We can't know until we visit them, or their citizens visit us. But we do think that from what little knowledge we have, intelligent life forms are not impossible on most of the nine planets.

Besides the possibility of life evolving to the point where intelligent creatures are possible, there is the possibility of such life forms migrating from another planet. Thus it is possible that on a planet that is completely barren a migrating race might have built dome cities, or cavern cities, and been living there for thousands or millions of years.

Gravity would hold no barrier to migrating peoples. For example, our own race could possibly migrate to a body having a surface gravity of a thousand times that here on Earth, and, if there were caverns far under the surface, could find a level where the weight of their bodies would be normal.

We have so little to go on in actual data to build a definite opinion on the posssibility of life on other planets in the solar system. We as yet don't know the actual beginnings of life, or under what conditions life could begin on a lifeless planet. It may be that when we do know, we can definitely say that life MUST exist on other planets.

It seems quite certain that intelligent life must exist in many places in the cosmos. It is quite probable that some of these races are much like our own, even close enough so that intermarrying would be possible! Probability dictates that such must be the case. But to find other intelligent races, if there are none other in our solar system, would be as hard as finding a particular grain of sand on the surface of Earth when its general location is not known. It might take millions of years of continual search.

And civilization is such a temporary thing. Our own has existed for only a few centuries, and there are indications that our race has been highly civilized several times before. It is possible that a century from now there will be no radio or printed matter, and no one who knows how to read. This bubble of science we have blown up might be shattered by a devastating war. So there might be intelligent races that don't have even the beginnings of science on several of the planets. Certainly a stellar visitor landing on earth a thousand years ago would have classed us as barbaric and unlearned. He might even do so today, if he glanced over our present theoretical science in current textbooks!

Turning to other sources of information than scientific speculation, we find that Mr. Shaver, Oahspe, and nearly all delvers into the occult positively state that other planets in our system have life on them, and also civilized creatures. From Oahspe it seems probable that not only is there civilized life on all the major planets, but that it is going through about the same course of evolution as our own.

The nearest sun to our own is Alpha Centauri, which is about four and a third light years distant. Our solar system goes about a fifth of a light year's distance in three thousand years. Yet, on page 128, verse 5, upper book, it says by implication that the other planets have life. "The holy council deliberated on the matters of the earth and her heavens, and all other corporeal worlds that were to pass through Don'ga for three thousand years, and it was found that the dawn of dan would fall upon the earth first of all."

That is the closest to a direct statement that I have been able to find in Oahspe concerning intelligent creatures on other planets in our solar system.

Shaver claims there are definitely people on some of the other planets. He claims they have space ship runs between the earth and the other planets.

There are hundreds of other sources that assert seriously and emphatically that space ships ply the interplanetary ways to and from our earth.

If that is so, why don't they make themselves known? Perhaps it is because we aren't civilized. Actually, we must be very backward in science relative to any race with the know-how of interplanetary travel. They have the vast laboratories of space in which to determine facts, while we have only the limited facilities of laboratories in a constant gravity field, and a strong one at that.

But since we don't know CERTAINLY that such travelers visit the earth, there is one more speculative possibility we must consider. It MIGHT be that no human being could live away from the planet, whatever the protection he might have. It might be that some of the complex molecules in our body would break down in other gravity fields and cause our death.

If that turns out to be so, then Oahspe's picture of a universe in which spirits ply the spaceways but not a single living creature does, a universe in which thousands of intelligent races live on as many planets and suns but do not migrate from one planet to another IN THE FLESH, would be a correct one.

Then, if and when the first explorers leave Earth for the moon or for Mars, they will never return. Or their ships will come back under robot control and we can see, perhaps, what killed the passengers.

Some day we may have the power and the know how to leave the planet—and the certain knowledge that to leave it is certain death. If it turns out to be the way then the only way you or I will ever visit Venus is to die. That's one angle—let's have more, so we can argue them out to whatever may be the truth, or as near as we can approach to it. What's the *evidence?*

The first five hundred subscribers to the club magazine have received a supplementary magazine along with this issue of the club publication. This supplemental magazine, SCIENCE COMICS, contains information pertinent to the Shaver Mystery, and was included for this reason. Only five hundred magazines were available, plus a few which are in the club library and will be loaned to any subscriber to read, and then return, for further loaning to others who did not receive the magazine.

A Preface and Forward to "Mandark" the Strangest thought provoking document ever to be published on our "world"

PREFACE

for people who like prefaces, and it's a long one—I warn you. But this book needs a preface if ever a book did.

* * *

THIS book is about the horror of Life today, and is the white root of truth about the forces that made our life the Hell it really is.

What lies behind these word-images, these figured letters—what is the Truth imprisoned in these symbols? If you can get it out, you will have more than any man has ever had from the written word. For there are vast implications, immense deductions which your brain will leap to, and be unable to refuse. There is a mighty chunk of knowledge here, but you cannot get it by ignoring it or sneering at it.

The ego sits—your ego—divorced from all reality by these myriad rows of strange symbols, by incomplete word images, by pictures you are supposed to make in your mind and will sometimes fail to, by the flickering phantoms of comings and goings which you call life. Life is a vague thing to most of us, *but it was not always so!*

The white root of the tree of life, the true meaning of the all-thought, reaches out and grasps these symbols as they pass before the eyes, putting into them the vital stuff of life. Your ego strives to understand, but FEARS to understand too often. Do not FEAR, but READ!

These fragile, evanescent blossoms of thought, from which all Man's works are constructed, what are they? They are the lure all men pursue. I, too, pursue the Lorelei that wakes us in the night and will not let us rest for reaching for her, that wraith for which our fingers curl in torment. The mother of these frail flowers, as strong as all the waterfalls of all the worlds, her it is I would know!

The universe is infinite in extent and all things are happening somewhere in the universe. Those mysterious barriers which the Mother of All Thought winds around the deadly lure of the white lightning of her body—that is where this story is written. Do not be *afraid* to understand.

Time and Man are two flows of opposite direction. Man from the past into the future, and time from the future into the past. But these things are only motile concepts. But it seems that energy is more motile than thought, and molds itself into all things, too. Our reality resides in our NOW. TIME is NOW, to Man.

Our ego is one point of NOW-light running over the assembled hosts standing in the darkness. It is a light with concentric rings of less and less brilliance. Into your eternal, too empty NOW I wish to put the hosts of the mighty, unknown beings of the far past, in a revealing detail which you have never encountered in accounts, and few they are, of these beings before.

To conquer one little NEW thought is a more important victory than to conquer the whole physical world without changing it for the better. I give you that opportunity.

Infinity is itself a vast and ready proof of the truths of this story.

If you grant the infinity of time and of space, as a non-stop expanse, then in that great magnitude of separate sets of conditions and circumstances favorable to various forms of life, in the infinite number of *Places* especially favorable to the full development of life in the infinitudes of space and time, there must have occurred at least once AN ESPECIALLY FAVORABLE PLACE! And there LIFE developed into a GOD-LIKE growth of beings infinitely greater than Man in powers of intelligence, strength, beauty and size.

Thus if we grant infinity, we must also grant the existence of beings so superior to man as to constitute a reasonable facsimile of our general concept of GOD.

If we grant the concept "infinity" as being reasonably accurate as a description of what we see when we look into the heavens, we have automatically accepted the existence of Gods.

Life has perhaps been developing great numbers of such beings and races of such beings in her endless stretches into times and spaces where we know nothing of what exists. Some of these beings, in the infinite numbers of the opportunities for them to do so, must have become immortal by mastering the great enemy—DEATH.

SINCE this must have happened by the laws of probability if the universe is big enough, then these GODS must have been very fecund, for a healthy immortal would certainly have children still living when he reached the age of a few thousand years.

Therefore, from the word "infinity" springs the certainty that there are God-like beings populating a large part of that infinity. It seems an unavoidable conclusion when we look up at the stars and think about probability laws. It would even seem probable, from the age of the earth, that some of these beings must have touched Earth at some time or other. For such beings must be so fecund, must fill so much of habitable space with their life that they must have set foot on Earth at some time for some purpose.

We have the legends of the Gods, and we have also other relics not so well known to tell us that this was so! We know, for instance, *why they are not here now!*

We know that the enemy of such life as we have concepted as God-life is those same stars that dot our night sky with their deadly light. Those stars are as deadly to life of all kinds as radium is deadly to all life. The immortals avoid all stars as we avoid the plague: for all stars, as well as our sun, are the cause of age! And the immortals prefer to live on.

Hence, if Earth was touched by the feet of the Gods, it was before Earth had a sun, or before Earth's sun was deadly as it is now. If that was so, then Earth was cold when they lived on it. Hence they must have lived deep inside Earth to avoid the cold and to take advantage of Earth's internal heat or to keep in the heat of their own fires by the insulation of the rock. If that was ever true, then in the deep rock of mother Earth must lie the traces of the God's life here.

Well, *I have been here!* Deep within the earth, and the traces are infinitely more than traces! There are, underneath our rocky surfaced Earth, cities in a great network from one to six miles deep and some much deeper. They are full of machinery of a kind too complex for men to understand, and no man as we know him ever built. People have lived and evolved in those abandoned God-homes since the earliest days of Man on earth. And they have kept their secret; not so much because they particularly wanted to keep it, perhaps. But because it has been impossible to tell incredulous Man anything about it, for he would not believe them when he was told. Few will fully believe this statement, but it is true!

The people who live there have evolved differently than Man on the surface. They are different, more different inside than out, mentally than physically. They know all about us, we know nothing of them. They have weapons superior to anything we can devise, built by the Gods themselves and abandoned in those ancient homes when the Gods left the sun-death of Earth for the clean dark spaces where no sun causes age.

This book tells something of the history of these hidden people, and of the history of the time when the Gods were on Earth, read from records deep in caverns.

This book is written by two people, though in truth a great many minds had something to do with it. The most important is one small person called Nydia of the Hidden People. Nydia does not write complicated English, not because she can't think that way, but because she was raised differently from we, of the surface. Moreover, she is blind, but she can talk and she knows a great deal more about the Hidden People than anyone else among them I ever met. She ought to know, she is one, and listened to and remembers all their oral history from the older people all her life. She doesn't know where she was born for sure, but it is somewhere under Massachusetts. She is an expert in a little-known science, the science of using apparatus built by minds of a vast superiority to the mind of man. She can even make repairs on machinery that a modern technician would fear to touch for fear of breaking it irreparably. She inherits the legends and word-of-mouth history of a people who have, unknown to Modern Man, been a hidden part of his life since the most ancient times. But I will write her idea of the beginning of this book and you can see for yourself whether an ordinary school-book education is necessary to an intelligent mind. Nydia was educated in a way that no modern man is educated whom you know—by reading telepathically the minds of many people since her early childhood.

NYDIA'S WORDS

I, NYDIA, am one of those who are born and live out their lives in the dark. Wretched is he whom the memories of childhood include always the miserable hiding of the self. Always the silence to those whom we want most to talk. Always the mysteries of education which are denied us. Always the happy faces of the surface people of the outer-world above going about their lives unmindful of us of the dark. I am like you others of the dark. I direct my words to you, too, in the hope that you will at last wake up from the sleep of ages of unnatural secrecy which has thwarted all our ancient aspirations for a world such as the Gods left us. I have been a miserable child, yet a busy one. I know not where I was born, for like so many of the underworld, we moved about so much a child could not know its birth-place. The hot, dry air of the caves was my air too, and the high arched ceilings of the God's lost homes were my home too. The magic "mech" were my toys, too, and always I watched the surface people and kept quiet as we are all taught. I was one of those who sometimes help the surface people and kept quiet. I was one of those who made mock and sport of them when I was a child, but I outgrew that, as many of us have outgrown the foolish sport of mocking people better than ourselves.

Always, I, too, feared the evil ones, the ignorant, degenerate and cannibalistic ray people who catch and kill us when they can. But they did not catch many of us, for we had some old ray women from the Deep Schools with us, and we were not easy to catch. But it is no wonder they sometimes catch and eat us, for there is so much help at hand which our antique custom of secrecy and hiding keeps us from using that our frequent fate at the hands of the stupid of the caverns is largely our own fault. Why should we be few when we can be many? But the customs were observed by me as by you, for in those days I did not think, but only obeyed. I played by myself, watching the surface of the far caves where the lovers sometimes wander and occasionally fail to return, as you know well. But love will be alone, even in the dark of the ancient caverns. And down here the food supply is none too abundant. We, who trade with the "holders" or the "watchers"—the old families of superior wealth who have always held the openings—look delicious, plump and irresistible to their empty stomachs fed on insects and cave snakes and fungi. They wait for one of us to show himself that they may feast.

Then, too it is no wonder we fall prey to such wandering ghouls. For do we not search for and sell the very weapons that would defend us against such creatures that only look like men—and do not do that very well? Where do these weapons we need so much and must sell for food go? Would it not be better to use these antique treasures than to sell them? Should we not use them to take the food we sell our all for now? Yes, it would be better if we made our way to the surface and used these weapons and wonder machines to dazzle and beguile the unknowing men of the surface into giving us food and homes in the sun?

But, like you, I cannot stand the sun. I would shrivel and die if I had to face that burning monster the surface people love so well! Yet something of the kind could be done, should be done, rather than sell the wonder treasure of our ancient homes to the men who come from space in the same kind of antique ships that lie unused in our own caverns because we have forgotten the ways of space flight, if our people ever knew those ways.

I WILL tell you why we do not do the things we should for our own safety. It is because the terrible evil that has always been a part of our life in the dark has gotten the upper hand. If our unwritten word-of-mouth history is any criterion it has had the upper hand for many centuries. Since those earliest days, when the goblins and ghouls of the dark homes of the lowest pits overwhelmed the wisdom of the hidden people, of the little people, of the troll people with their numbers, their stupid destructiveness their lust to kill, since the time the legends picture as Ragnarok or Armageddon or what-have-you when the frost giants and monsters of the lost lands of the dark whelmed at last the light of wisdom that was Aesir, whelmed in the south the wisdom that was Faery, whelmed in the East the kind underworld that was Peri and other names, since those days when there were really wise ray people that were not mad and evil.

Evil has ruled the underworld except for small areas of better intended rule. We don't know just why this evil became ascendant in the Elder world, but since the death of Christ from the "dill-headed" work of the evil hidden ones, since the fall of Rome, our life has been evil, and we have come to accept all the burden of evil as our customs, our hard and fast laws. Our hiding, our secrecy, our tremendous power never used any more for anything but to make our own life more miserable. Sometimes it is sold to outlander spacemen. All these customs that make up our way of life, the stim palaces that consume and infect our youth, all the repression that keeps us ignorant and vice-ridden, are the result of the evil of the past and what it has done to our minds. We must shuck our evil! We must cast off the old ways and start anew.

We must do so in order to bring about a result that would insure a great fortune for Man. A future different from the hideous darkness of the past, for which in many ways secret ray men were responsible and in many ways our secret ignorance too is responsible. I have worked with these surface men to prepare this book. It is not a perfect book, but it will serve our purpose. The minds of the surface men are not easily made receptive to these truths of the ancient mechanism and its long use in the caverns, but what I have told them they have adopted into a story about their Christ, whom so many of us laugh at, and the Christians who are so often the special butts of our worst jokes, of our cruelest deeds upon the defenseless surface men. This story exists in truth on the old thought-records, poor records they are, made long after the time by the evil ones—but still true thought-records in which the story of that time can be made out.

THE ones I help now have also written of the people who built the caves, and the machines I have shown them. Yes, some of them were down here, but I could not let them stay for long, for you know what our customs are. What they have written of the past is true and taken straight from the most antique records of the ancient times I could find for them. You who know about such things may not need this book, but to you who wallow in ignorance in the worst of the caverns—I tell you, read it, and take the many hints left for you about the mechanisms and about its use, about the sun and its nature, about evil and its cause and its ways. So, have a wise man read it over your telemachs, and listen well, for you will learn things you will find useful and have things explained that have puzzled you always.

In the book there are a few accounts of the past, the very far past, as the wiser of we hidden people know of it, and a forecast of what our future may be if we circumvent this evil. You of the underworld will at last understand why evil exists and why it is, and mayhap how best to fight it. And you of the surface, knowing now that we below you exist, that we of the ancient deeps called the Elder world still exist as we did in the ancient legends and still use the same old magic that is described in those old tales, hayhap will acquire some of the antique magic and ferret out the wondrous science that lies waiting in the intricacies of the workings of those miraculous and indestructible ancient machines.

If you do re-discover the ancient wisdom, the future of Man will again approach the immortal and glorious past. Man will defeat his worst enemy, age. For that mighty, impossible people who built these vast caverns were immortal and these caverns contain the secrets of that immortality. Man will defeat his vile seducing master, Evil—him he will cast off for good. Men will grow great again as were the wise Gods of the far past of the wide spaces.

That these things may come to pass some day, long after we are dead and this book has spread and grown into other books about the caverns, and time has made of the contents of this book a living force in the minds of men—many minds of many men and not a few hidden miserables like ourselves—this book is written.

I know that words alone cannot accomplish this wonder work—but words can do wonder work when they grow alive as thought in many mens' minds. If you of the underworld take them to your heart as you have taken other teachings in the far past, if you will again love Man enough to try for him one more time—mayhap we will succeed even though we are no longer truly men as the ancients thought of men. To a time such as the fabled "Golden Age", to the time that will exist again when men can live in love and wisdom and real happiness such as we of the caves know can be but surface men do not comprehend; to that time these words and this life are dedicated.

Nydia.

THE other person who worked on this book is known as Richard S. Shaver. He knew Nydia, a child of what is called a "witch", a child of the nomadic life of the hidden caverns; and for many years they planned such a book together. At last it became a reality.

Shaver visited the caves by the help of Nydia and, while there, read some of the infinitely important ancient records of the Elder race who built the endless cavern cities that still lie deep in the under-rock of our planet. The rest of this tale of Man's past he pieced together with Nydia's help, and it is perhaps the truest account of the origin of Man in existence.

It is not a fantastic confection, though many will think so. It is, in truth, a history put up as a series of dreams, in order to convey that there is more value in such visions recorded by prophets and others in the Bible and similar books than one is apt to believe. There is no guessing in our way of thinking of past time "when" these caverns came into existence or how many centuries passed before Man, as we know him, re-discovered them, only to keep that discovery a monopoly of a few.

The result of this book, if you understand, is to upset your whole concept of the past of Man as well as the scientist's guesses at the origin of animal life upon Earth— and much of the plant life too. It shows that Earth is not so old *under the sun* as the scientists contend, and that the old legends and fairy tales, so long discredited as mere childish entertainment by historians and similar writers, have more truth in them than most of the serious writings of the same writers. In fact, they are more accurate in a broad way than the technical gentlemen's guesses at the unknown past. If you can throw aside, for a time, everything you have been taught of the past and read this book with an open, unangered mind, you will never get the old erroneous ideas back. Not many will be able to do this, perhaps, but they will get a great story anyway.

The book is really an actual account of a terrific experience with the unknown. The men of the under-world who loved Nydia, opened their hearts to get Shaver out of a predicament that was proving fatal. Nydia rescued Shaver and, to hide him, let him into the long forbidden life of the caves. The result in this book, and you can believe it or not, but you can't disprove it! No matter how many masters of the written word this book contradicts, you cannot prove it wrong. For there are endless corroborations of the basic facts of this book to be found in old writings, and some of these you will find in a special section in the back of the book. Students will argue over these corroborations for centuries, but they won't be able to discredit a one of them. For the caves have always existed, and their magic has played a part in history since before the Pharaohs rode out to conquer the Ethiopians, since before Merlin used such magic to aid King Arthur, since before Moses defeated the might of the Pharaoh and released the Jews from bondage.

The Greeks knew the Gods in Homer's time, and worshipped them. We have forgotten why they thought there were Gods, but they had a reason—a reason that still exists today, but the reason is not God-like today. When a man hears voices today, we put him in a mad-house. In the old days, they said he "talked to the Gods", or in some periods that he was "possessed" or "bewitched". They were *all* right, in part! A greater truth is here!

I, DICK SHAVER, have read some of those antique records, some of which are perfectly preserved in their sealed, airtight cases. I am going to tell a story I read within those records, for you so that you can see what an educated man of the caverns is. He is a man who has lived lives beyond anything you of the surface can conceive, whose education, though fragmentary, is often the thought of the Gods, the Elder race, themselves.

So they are different from you in many ways, though the educated people of the caves are few and our education nothing that you can grasp as such. Some of them do not know multiplication tables, but CAN operate teleportation machines that will send matter over a beam through the rock for miles. It is incredible, but so are those machines built by an incredible race. So is "infinity" incredible, yet there it is above us every night. They had such machines, and they built imperishably. Levitators were the simpler machines they used for building work and other necessary lifting. The more complicated machinery is entirely incomprehensible in principle, but it is possible still to use some of them. Much of the apparatus was designed primarily for pleasure, their children went through a much longer play period than our own, and the play machines are numerous and vast, and much of it is evidently for the great-bodied adults' recreation, as well. Their pleasure palaces still exist today, and are what Coney Island would be if it were built by a race possessing millions of minds each a million times as able as our own.

They do not ask surface people to visit them, for even if surface men heard the "voice" they would fear it. It takes years of contact to remove the fear and make of a surface man a ready friend or servant. Too, their customs are such that a person entering would be next thing to a slave. We of the surface would not want that, and they do not ask us. A smothering blanket of fixed custom hovers over all the underworld work and life and little good comes from under that blanket. How to break these age old bonds that hold the antique wisdom from useful development as a part of the life of surface men is my life problem. I do not write well, perhaps, but I am giving you an honest effort, toward the awful truth of the mightier past and the vaster possibilities for the future than you will find in any other writer. Of the things I speak, make an effort to accept before you refuse me. I know the truth, please see it.

* * *

FOREWORD

REALITY—*is it a horror?*

To all you young idealists there will come a time when all those things you think of Life with your bright, trusting and believing eyes will become dust and slime. A time when you will understand the terrible and stupid horror that life may be, in reality.

Life is a scream in the face of a mad brightness, then! Life is a silly sound like a death rattle from an insane clown dying in the night, then.

Life is a place where the books still preach that death and morbid foolishness and churchyard fears and opened graves are sense. That to shiver at ghost stories and to half-believe in them is not foolishness.

Life is a place where all you have learned as sound wisdom is not wisdom at all when you come to a need to use that wisdom.

Because there *is* in truth a supernatural something that mocks at life.

When you meet, face to face, that something that comes and goes through locks and bars and wisdom's pale fences of flimsy, unsound logic you learn that this thing is a powerful stupidity that mocks all your bright ideals with a smothering, mad will in the night, a will that takes your best out of your body and leaves a nothing in you that yet wants to live more—but is afraid to live.

To each of you will come at last an apparition, wearing like Scrooge, his chains, a mask of terror that hides a deep basic stupidity—a dumbness that is deeper than human.

Then like ignorant medieval people you will believe in elemental spirits, but it is not so!

They have life, those things, just as you have life; but they are not understood and are so terribly feared that men will neither speak of them or write of them openly, but always with a hedge of protection, a flimsy barricade of fiction to hide their belief from men who do not believe—OR IS IT TO HIDE THEIR KNOWLEDGE FROM THE THING ITSELF?

"They" ARE talked of openly only between men who *do* know them and know that the other knows, too. Mostly these men think of them as witches and warlocks and such foolishness of the weak mind of men.

I give you the open truth. It is not pretty. But it is wise to know this truth, and not stumble upon his horror unprepared only by the works of the "learned" idiots who have never experienced "Fortean" phenomena.

BESIDE this horror that exists mysteriously—there is also the horror that is the plain face of Life itself, when looked at in certain revealing lights.

To all young men and women who dream will come at last the awful dream that is the *face of truth*. A true vision will show them Life as a morbid horror, and themselves as a mad man-speck upon Earth's surface as a fly upon paper. This is the DIS-illusion, and I give you an armor of proof against it. That armor is an exact, obviously correct explanation of what this DIS-illusion consists.

You will need this armor on that day when you know that you are a living thing that must die because your feet are so firmly fastened in the mud of Earth. That you must die and gasp out your life at the last without ever attaining one bright fulfillment of one brave dream. We must each one day look upon this awful face of Truth.

When that time comes and you know that yourself is the man who is growing old and shaky and that all those things you have worked away your life to accomplish will never become to you anything but a sad waste of the bright hours of your lifetime—that day you will be infinitely glad you have read this book. That day you will need the bright light of this book "Mandark" to save you from leaping thankfully into death.

*   *   *

Mandark tells you why Life *seems* a darkness, why reality is a fearful thing we turn our minds away from. For there *is* something in life to work for if enough people can be brave and wise. But somehow we never have the leaders of broad and swift vision to lead us to the reality of those things we know are best—but somehow never strive toward—because we are led toward more futile, life-wasting efforts.

Mandark, if understood, can set you free of DIS-illusion.

Then when you see the green, dull face of Death mouldering, your wisdom can face it with a face as brightly laughing as the face of a child.

We know the child laughs only because it does not know that life is only a doorway to death. That life brings always death.

For our life seems even to our wisest men, by their writings, but a fertilizing for the dark fields of death. That our life has been before, and can be again, much more than that, they do not see.

THE awfulness of Truth's sad face that peers out at we who write of reality—and are called madmen, liars and various other names less attractive for reminding men that reality has vastly more to it than the bright foolish image in a kitten's eyes—that they do not see.

Or that the eyes of a drunken youth recognize only those things the youth wishes to see—and that all youth is so drunk with life-energy as to notice only that drunken untruth. Men do not wish to think of dying until they must.

How then can Death be argued with if men fear to face him with direct, courageous thought?

The reality says life travels only to death, and all the maundering of the religious calling on heaven as their witness (as if they could ever *believe* that heaven really existed) calling on the goodness of a God who (they say) is cognizant of Earth and all Earth's madness and all our need of the things that a God would supply—seems only to prove to the wise and honest man that there is no God—that religious people are either liars or madmen.

This "God" that does nothing that we can see but commiserate us through the mealy mouth of a mockingly unbelieving and obviously lying religion-preacher and priest—all our lives this "God" of theirs mockingly ignores all our needs.

And we wait in our terrible need for the work of this "God" and get instead the loud daily shouts of hypocrites or madmen over our radios and out of their pulpits.

When one speaks of this with honest, careful words one hears shouts of "liar" from these self-same liars— as if a "God" existed anywhere who is responsible for this mad mess, our Earth life.

The other Gods would kill him the first whiff of a concentration camp, the first smell of the smoke of a Nazi slaughter camp; he cannot exist—if God exists at all!

With all the mealy mouths of mad preachers telling us sadly that when we die we will be made to play upon a harp up in the incomparable land within the Pearly Gates, and that the misery of life is explainable as a testing of something or other that none of them has ever seen, but which they are all quite ready to swear exists—the soul—what is an honest man to do?

That the misery of life is explainable as a testing of a something none of them has ever seen or can ever demonstrate to exist, yet of course they believe in it—sure they do—pass the plate, suckers.

The sad, mad face of our ancient pagan mother earth, that ghost who still has demonstrable power. Witness: who does bear up our feet?—who is the biggest thing in sight?—what great mother can take the searing rays of sunlight and make them into the sweet magic of a May morning for children and sweethearts and puppies and wise old men who love their mother earth?—what does *she* think of them who deny her?

This book contains the dark truths of Hell, as well as the bright faces of the true Gods of the past. It will leave you better armored to face the rigors of courageous seeing of the realities of "life".

MANDARK

By RICHARD S. SHAVER

Beginning a 200,000 word Novel - The true Thought-Record Story of the Life of Christ

CHAPTER I

THE DREAM

ONCE I was just a person as you probably are. Then one hot night I had a dream. Let me tell you that dream and what it did to me.

Under the kneed cypress trees the lilies sway softly; red are their faces, and their leaves . . . *black*. Their anthers protrude like the tongues of little snakes, darting quickly from side to side. The poisonous white pistil writhes as though in pain of waiting, waiting like the single fang of the horn snake, poised to pour forth death. The cypress limbs drip soft grey sounds and slow winds coil through the shrouding mist. The heavy orchids lean their faces to be seen, their dangling roots white and vague like unseen thoughts that have yet to feel life. Their blooms are purple and gold with light pale stalks of green mottled with the swamp death. The black water ripples silently, heavily. Under the rings of ripples move the gaping mouths of great serpents, hungry for life to engulf. The acids of despair seem to distil slowly down the great stalks of starving plants.

Groping through the mist, her whitely gleaming flanks spattered with the green mud, her hair hanging like wild flames over her firm young breasts, comes Nydia! About her the vast and swaying silence of the swamp, the slow rustle of the curving leaves, the gentle stretching of the reaching tendrils, the heavy, subtle scent of the slow poison that is the breath of the swamp, the touching of the pale leaves to her shrinking skin—all seemed too loud a thing . . . weighed with fear, for such is flight.

No more would she preside at the hidden festivals of the Dark One.[1] The time when she was looked up to as the receptacle of the lore of the Ancients was gone. Now the Dark One, whom she had served so long, was called a Devil and his servitors were hunted as Witches or Sorcerers.

* * *

Now I was no longer the living and poisonous mist of some swamp caressing the muddy flanks of a fleeing witch, but was a man myself turning a corner into a darkened street.

There was a strange and furtive quietness about these streets, the gloom was thick

---

[1] *To you men who still worship and prostrate yourselves before the Dark Spirit of SATAN, and take the childish pranks and wistless cruelties of unseen beings as the work of Satan's spirits, I say: It is not true!*

There is no magic, only the existence of a lost science that built great mechanisms that can still cause phenomena that seem magic even to modern minds. But they are NOT magic. Many of those machines could be built by today's science did modern Man's mind happen to turn in that direction. To you who serve the under-world, THE ELDER WORLD, I Say: Serve those men of the darkness who serve the future and to Hell with the mummery and secrecy of the past. Serve science, even the seeming child's science of the surface world, and the results will be vastly more valuable than all the mummery and stim of the witches of Evil.

Free man from the curse of the ancient black magic forever, give him the workings of those antique mechanisms and let his science reproduce the wonders of the far past once again. Why do you still hide all that light under the secrecy that has shrouded the greatest wonders of Earth life from the man of the past?

Well, it shall not shroud the wonder that must be in the future! It shall contribute its mighty part. That mech in the caves must be studied by modern science, and must be no longer wholly hidden. Why have you not done this, if you think, men of darkness?

Illustration by Richard S. Shaver depicting life in the caves as he knew it.   Each detail of the picture exists as shown, according to Mr. Shaver.   The front cover by another artist, also depicts life in the caves.

and viscous, filled with a summer sensuality, as of a great, night-blooming flower's heavy odor. A woman's white face floated before me, the dark red lips hanging like moist fruit, her teeth gleaming. A husky whisper importuned, and I followed . . . Nydia.

The air was heavy with my sensual thinking, or was it the thinking of the whole city? A dark and ancient and red being permeated these houses and streets, a hanging odor of coiling, strangling caresses, of strange orgies and stranger visions. Every past image of the desired bodies of women, all women I had ever known stretched out their hands to me, and writhed gleaming limbs in a slow dance of longing, holding their red tipped breasts tightly with their spread hands as though to keep the growing buds from blooming suddenly into some wild flowering of culmination—and all their faces were . . . Nydia.

I awoke and lay there for a long time and dawn slowly brightened my window. All my mind was occupied with wonder—who *was* this Nydia?

AS I said before, once I was just such a person as yourself. I thought that people were lying and preachers were raving or lying when they said they saw God, or angels, or ghosts; when they said they had been hexed, or jinxed or heard voices they couldn't explain.

Then this dream happened. It was a lush, a terrible dream of a witch with whom I was apparently in love. I had been reading about such a witch, called "The Watcher", who had been active in medieval Spain.

During the dream I had thrashed about, it seemed, either in fear or in an attempt to follow the floating face of . . . Nydia. During the bodily activity of the dream, I must have overturned my urinal, which was in the usual place in country homes, under my bed. We called it a pot, or a "thundermug". The liquid spread over the solid-color brown linoleum, and spread in a large puddle about six feet by four beside my bed. The next morning when I awoke, the urine had dried, and upon it was a vivid photograph of the witch I had thought existed only inside my mind in the dream!

I knew enough about chemistry to know that a large number of chemicals will respond in a similar way to silver salts if conditions are right. Evidently conditions had been very right, and the only light that had struck that urine before it had dried in the darkness had been the image of the witch. I knew that some one, some way, had been foisting actual projections of the image of a witch upon my sleep as a dream. It is a strangely vivid dream that leaves a life size photograph upon the floor for a souvenir.

I called my friend from the next room. I said: "Do you see it?" and pointed at the photograph upon the floor.

"Yes", he answered, "I didn't know you were an artist. But isn't it a disgusting medium?"

"I didn't draw the damn thing," it is an actual photograph of a dream of a witch I had last night. How in Hades do you explain it?"

He didn't believe me, and after the urine was cleaned away we both refrained from speaking of the weird occurrence. He from a fear that I would be thought slipping my mental moorings, and I from a fear that I was.

Eventually I forgot the thing. But it left a peculiar doubt of life's accepted beliefs in my mind. The pragmatic base of my life, I thought, had been severely shaken.

Well, keep your feet on the ground. It wasn't a "ghost" that had inadvertently photographed itself upon my floor. The phenomena originated in the work of a *living person*, right enough. But when I finally learned of the mischievous elfin visitor, and her incredible history and background, where she lived and where her kind came from . . .

THE next occurrence on my path to a strange and terrible discovery of my hidden visitors who were to become both my friends and my enemies, the secret evil and as secret kindnesses hidden from our supposedly sane modern life, happened just as simply, from as common, vulgar things around me which suddenly opened upon a terrible vista of unknown life . . .

I was working in the factory.[2] It was the original Ford plant in Highland Park, Detroit. Some of the men there will remember me. Overhead conveyors shot diagonally across the spaces which are the light wells, around me were welding jigs, and every few

---

[2] *Norse legends of clever dwarves who could build anything—flying ships, Thor's hammer, etc. How else could this be done except in the Elder race machine shops? I have seen some terrifically complex weaving machines: shuttles like little metal hands on rods, etc.*

seconds I had to duck a welding gun. Two of them hung on swivels and were used in succession for two different sizes and shapes of welds. This swinging gun timed our action, gave a pulsating rhythm to our movements—but no matter.

I was the man doing the welding. I grabbed the gun as it swung, welded, pushed it away and ducked its mate as it swung into position over me, then straightened and shot the juice to the next weld. It gets tiresome after awhile, and when you forget to duck, you get a crack on the head from the heavy gun. When the "funny stuff" began, at first I thought it was the occasional bump on the head that had me slap-happy. But the hearing came only with one of the guns, so that ruled that out.

I began to notice something very strange about one of the guns. Whenever I held it, I heard voices, faroff voices of endless complexity. When I changed to the other gun of the pair, I heard nothing. Then I grabbed the gun again as it came around, and right away I knew what was in Bill's lunch box; which girl Bumpy was going to take out that night; what Hank's mother was planning on for his wife. It was a dress, and quite a dress too. More, I knew what the men upstairs were griping about; I heard everything I didn't want to hear all over the factory. That welding gun was, by some freak of its coils' field atunements *not* a radio, *but a teleradio:* a thought augmenter of some power. After awhile I found I could read the thought of nearly everyone in the building, if they were standing near the wires leading to my gun from the transformers off upstairs. For several hundred feet I was a Dunninger of the mind, and I fooled plenty of the fellows by telling them what they were thinking. But at last it began to get on my nerves . . . I'll tell you why: I began to hear "thought"! I couldn't figure it out. I would hear a mean kind of "voice" say:

"Put her on the target."

Then I would hear a woman's screams, louder and louder and more and more agony in the screams—and at last a gurgle, a death rattle. Then later I would hear some person thinking about a space ship; not a *new* spaced ship, but an *old* one—one *he had been out in space with!* What he thought about it was too much for me, but he knew plenty about electrics that I didn't.

I would hear a woman cursing and the lash of a whip—and feel a pleasure in the scream of the person getting the lash. It was all so mad, but I kept hearing such things, over and over. It got on my nerves, so I quit. I quit and went on the bum, for I didn't feel like working any more, because I believed—I *knew*—I heard the voices and that if that was what telepathy gave a man to hear in America, I wasn't going to work for America. I was a *smart guy*—and pretty soon I was running a liquor truck between Detroit and Toledo. Easy money, and I had the satisfaction of knowing I wasn't a sucker for any hidden bunch of devils like I figured was running America, from what I heard.

Well, so far I haven't said much, but wait—and I'm not telling you any fancy lies either. You may think so for awhile, till you see what I'm driving at.

Well, like all smart guys, I wound up with a lot of iron bars around me, which wasn't too bad, till I began to hear "thought" again without a welding gun within miles of me. Then for a while I *knew* I was nuts! I kept it quiet. I didn't say a word about it. If I was insane, I figured it was my business. Then I began to feel pains, and the thought in my head kept laughing at me. Like an imp from hell[3] would laugh.

---

[3] *To walk and know that every step is watched by a mad thing, a thing without thought except to harm, to torment, to kill—a thing with the vast and mysterious weapons of a God at his fingertips, and the brains of a blood-crazed fish—that is the life of luckless individuals who know the truth of the ancient caverns in which such things live!*

That has been the fate of certain luckless individuals since earliest times on Earth. It is supposed to be the fate of those who might divulge the ancient secret, but the mad ones as often as not torment ignorant innocents.

Many men who could have told this story better than I, did not; because "men are happier not knowing the hopeless truth", or because "they feared this fate of the 'follower'". They have had many names; Maupassant called them "The Horla."

But I think that those who know and yet take this defeatist attitude are wrong. Once it may have been better not to know that the efrits, demons and goblins and what-not whom some heard and talked to were real living fleshly beings—not spirits at all. Today there are many, as there were in the dark ages, who know something of these terrible truths of the past that still live to plague and waste man-life.

But today is different. This modern man has the beginnings of a science that may one day eclipse the Elder science by far. Those beginnings are not to be squandered by the madness, the maundering cruelties of unseen things who have no true mind.

THE pains got worse. Finally I knew what it was, but I didn't believe it. It was people living caves under and around the prison, and the people's kids liked to torment us prisoners! Not just pester, but real, genuine torture, done with some kind of X-rays. At last I got mentally used to knowing this, for I finally got wise to a couple of other sufferers from the unseen rays, and we would get off in a corner and discuss the thing. So I didn't feel so alone, or so nuts about it all.

We all knew that something was very wrong about ordinary people's ideas of what the world was like. I realized that modern science must have developed a lot of secret things that rich people had got hold of and were keeping from common people. I finally was quite sure I knew all about the "crooked secret ray" business. But I was wrong! How wrong that idea that "modern" science was responsible for my misery was!

I figured maybe the communists were right. At last after what seemed like centuries of torment, but was really less than two years, something happened that was the *best* thing that ever happened to me.

A change came over the people in the caves, of whom we only knew through their rays. Somebody got their number and really began to make them behave. I figured the law-men got hold of some of the "ray" and were giving them what-for. But I was wrong again.

One result of the change was a sudden access of "pleasure" rays. I learned that for every *pain* ray, those secret people had a dozen infinitely *pleasant* rays. They called it stim,[4] and woke me every morning with floods of the most delicious sensations on earth. Stim is like a young girl's kiss augmented by magic to a million powers. One of the young ray people was a girl who seemed to fall for me. She especially dished out this stim ray to me. There is no value on earth so great as stim love. Her name was Nydia.

Our love became a great, overpowering force, that ruled us day and night. It could not go on apart, and she was not going to let it. But, of course, I was mad and dreaming by day, as well as by night. For this happened . . .

One night about 1 A.M. my cell door opened! I sat up, astonished. What did the screws want with me this time of night? But the turnkey stood just outside the door, a dazed, *zombie* expression on his face. I thought he was walking in his sleep till I saw behind him the transparent image, the half-existent projection, I had learned to love as "my girl" of the "secret people." The luscious, laughing face of my friend resolved my mind of worry or astonishment, it was all just "play" to her. But to me it was the door to freedom. She wasn't there in person, but the next best thing, a transparent projection of herself. I was going to her, I knew!

By controlling rays[5] of the mechanism of their secret science, she had imposed

---

[4] *Around Nydia was all the machinery of a God's pleasures. The very air could be saturated with both nutrient vapor and beneficial vibrants, as well as vibrants designed purely for pleasure, as is our music of "sounds." The nature of these vibrants I can best describe by telling you that the stimulation you receive from the embrace of the woman you love is due to the body electric that the millions of tiny batteries which are the body cells give off.*

The Titan and Atlan (the two main Elder races) scientists could and did synthesize all such vibrants and many others for which the machinery still exists. A great many of their mechanisms exist still in the deep, so-called "hidden" caverns, and are in use today, for the machines were built of imperishable metals, and many such machines are sheathed in solid gold. No words can describe the pleasure which a room full of these various vibrants, or synthetic pleasure nerve waves, can give a mere man. Multiply the embrace of the finest woman, you know by a million powers, and you have a vague idea of the Nirvana which the Titan and Atlan races accepted as normal living conditions. A far cry from our "heating stove" was the apparatus around which the Titan's family gathered.

[5] *This antique device has been used since pre-historic times by the hidden peoples to produce the phenomena called Possession. Possessed of a devil, Spirit Possession, etc.*

It is a conducive ray of similar nature to the short wave electric flows which are our nerve messages and our thought. Manufactured by the mechanism to bear the messages of thought from the origin to receptor, they can be used to super-impose such thought upon a man's mind and body in such strength that his body and his mind do as the thought message dictates, for it is far stronger in quantity than the product of his own mind and nervous energy. It is still so used today, but the luckless "murdered by control" today has no such excuse of "possession" as was used in medieval times. He just says he didn't know what he was doing and let's it go at that. Nor could he say more, for today it is called "insanity" to mention the underworld, or any of what are called "supernatural" phenomena. Yet these phenomena are present to some extent in every man's life, but the fashion of recognizing them as such has changed, for the worse.

her thoughts upon the mind of the turnkey in such strength that his own were powerless, being so much weaker. Merely by thinking over the ray with the terrific augmentation of the secret thought-radio, she made the unconsious screw unlock the door of the cell. He led me to a little-used side door, and let me out into the night unobserved by anyone else.

Then that ghostly imp-angel took me by the hand and led me for miles deep into the wooded countryside. Within a thick grove she led me to a great gap in the rocky hillside. As I followed her transparent young form, behind me a vast door swung shut with a weird shriek. If love hadn't had me bemused, I would have been plenty scared, for I was in truth following a ghost into the interior of a small mountain. I knew that no one would know there was a door there, now that it was closed.

The dim light inside the caves I found emanated from long tubes running alongside cavern walls. The cavern was alien, vast sculptured rock-forms of beings not human upheld the high, carved arches of the roof that was a mountain overhead. The tubes contained some self-activating material which glowed. Once, it was probably productive of a strong light but now it gave off a dim glow. The girl sensed my thoughts and spoke: "In other of the caverns there is brilliant light which can be switched on and off."

Into this twilight the ghostly little figure continued to draw me. We emerged at length into a vast room, around which could be dimly seen huge mechanisms of incomprehensile uses. Beside one of these stood a soft, utterly enticing figure that was the duplicate of the phantom that had led me here. The screen still glowed brightly from use.

As my footsteps rang on the ancient polished stone floor, this little figure raced toward me unerringly and threw herself into my arms. Her flower-red mouth sought mine like a starved animal scenting meat. As she left the receptor screen of the ancient mechanism, the phantom beside me disappeared abruptly.

"Dick, my poor love. You are with me at last! It has seemed so long." Her voice was music to me who had starved so long for the tender tones of this woman's voice. My arms went about her slender child's form. I leaned my face to those questing lips and learned more about love in two seconds than all the past of my life had taught me. The little witch had left the augmentor beam on me and only those who have loved under those ancient impulse augmentors can undrstand the terrific depths of love. I knew that I had never really lived until that fierce moment when our love sprang into flaming life.

At first I felt sure that Nydia could see me, her intent wide eyes were fixed on me so surely. But she said:

"Almost I see you; you seem much bigger, now that you are here. My mind can see you, in a way that you will learn too."

I knew now that Nydia was blind!

I looked about for the first time. I realized that little sweetheart was but poorly clad, not at all like the projection she had made of herself into my prison cell. I learned later that that projection she had made of herself into my prison cell was largely mental, so that her likeness went clad as she would have liked to be clothed. In reality, her garments were but a few well-worn rags. I myself could have wished I wore less than my prison denim; for the temperature was high, as it is in deep mines. Her fair hair, her large unseeing eyes, her paper-white skin, were as I had seen them in my prison.

THE vast round space where we stood was surrounded by hulking, mysterious machines; they stood dimly gigantic in the faint light of the cavern lamps.

I asked Nydia where her people were. She said with a little laugh that they were leaving us to ourselves at this moment of our meeting, but that I should meet them soon enough.

"Oh, Dick, in many ways they are different from surface folk, and you must not let these differences disturb you. They are prepared to welcome you heartily because I love you and they love me. But it is not our custom to admit surface people to our hidden ways, for they are so apt to fear us and thus hate and be a danger to us. Greet them naturally and show no fear or repulsion no matter how they look to you. We are different from the kind of human you are used to. We need men like you to aid us in our constant struggle with the living devils that inhabit much of these underground warrens. But when we try to approach men for this purpose, they fear the whole thing as madness or ghosts or whatever they have been taught. You see, we are forced to fight the devils because we wish evil to no one and cannot be glad when others suffer, and that is a way of life that all the evil and degenerate nomad bands hate and seek to destroy."

The space within the mountain was an Aladdin's cave, beautiful beyond a modern man's imagination. The hall where Nydia next led me, saying it was a hall where the group met for any social purposes, was pillared by mighty metal simulations of trees, hung with crystalline, jewel-like fruit. In every one of these great rooms stood several of the enigmatic ancient mechanisms, themselves beautiful of form and shimmering with prismatic color.

Some of the machines had a startling way of talking; when one neared them they would speak in a strange tongue, beautiful sounding words of a meaning incomprehensible. That is a strange sensation, hearing a machine speak to you. I suspect they were equipped to announce their need of oil or other minor adjustment, as we equip mechanisms with red lights to indicate need for adjustment.

The solid, gleamingly polished floor of rock was inlaid with weirdly beautiful designs and writings in symbols which I deduced were from the ancient's lost language—verses, perhaps. Imperishable metal lounges, once probably covered with the "shining fabrics which the Gods alone could weave", stood beside the gleaming, ancient "mech" as the cavern people call the old machines.

From the great machinery cavern she led me into a smaller room, a strange mixture of metal super-work, and old hand-made wooden furniture that must have been brought into the room comparatively recently, though still centuries ago. We sat on a wooden bench that was half a log, split and with heavy oak pegs for legs. She told me of her people; they were but few, only fifty or so living in the terrific abandoned splendor of the forgotten race who had built this God-home. They had perhaps not read many books, though there were some modern books about. But they had read men's minds over the telaug beams that penetrated the miles of the rock of the hills overhead and was so conductive and augmentive one could read a man's mind with them *many miles away.* In some ways they knew more of life than does the ordinary man by far. It was not till later that I learned the fearful depths of their knowledge.

They had at different times contacted surface people and tried to persuade such of them as were intelligent and able to join them. But they had been rebuffed from fear that their soft invitation to their mysterious retreat masked a snare or was a mental delusion.

"It is always so," they would say, and shrug. "For those men who know of the ancient secret of the hidden people know also of the evil it has always done, and hence fear all who handle the rays, though many are wise and good and try to nullify the evil and reduce the torments inflicted by the degenerate and mad nomads of the caverns."

Of the fifty in this group there were no such evil people. Many of the cavern people came of clean and ancient stock that has striven for centuries to make the magic of the caverns the property of surface scientists, of use to everyone.

AGES of life in the dark had developed their senses in ways variant to surface folk. They had very large eyes, with great pupils adapted for sight in darkness, and over the long-range sensitive sight beams of the ancient ray mechanisms. Their skins were either a light brown, or a paper white, or a mottled, strangely lumpy appearance that comes of a fungus skin disease peculiar to the caverns. But under their strange exteriors there beat most warm and human hearts, and they opened these hearts to me because of Nydia's affection for me. A friend of Nydia, their little "wisdom-worker" was a friend of theirs.

They had a complete comprehension of the terrific significance of the ancient secret of the God-caves mechanisms and the value of a knowledge of their uses.

But it is not, after all, so many years ago when all such people were burned as witches or sorcerers. They had a hearty fear of surface peoples' bungling hands getting hold of their way of life and ruining their freedom and their secret power completely. The fact that rickets is not common among them I attribute to the fact that the ancient race who built the ray mechanisms included a supply of those actinic rays which defeat tuberculosis and rickets and similar afflictions. They were, in truth, quite healthy. Their health I attribute to their constant use of the ancient rays for one purpose or another, and those rays were built to be beneficial. Their great mental quickness is also due to this factor, as well as to the telaug use, which accustoms them to handling great volumes of thought from many minds.

Nydia, not alone among her kind, had vast plans and ideas for the future. She urged more surface contact for the purpose of developing a more intelligent use and understanding of the ancient science which had built the miraculous mechanisms. She had at last fallen in love with me, a surface man and brought me with her into her cavern home.

Among the cavern people, marriage is purely a personal matter; people either live together or do not, and it is no one else's business. I often think their attitude in this respect is the correct one. In the caves, when two people promise themselves to each other, they keep their promises—which is more than I can say for surface life. Nydia spent exactly one week showing me that what happened to Tannhauser in the Hollow Hill of the Venusberg with Venus can still happen to mortal man. She had studied the uses of the antique pleasure ray mechanisms under masters, some of whom I met later. And for one week I experienced all the pleasures of a God's nuptials; tremendous stimulation generators poured super-powered pleasure impulses through every nerve of my body at full capacity. If a man could die of pleasure, I think I would have died.

But my tender-hearted Nydia was no slave of pleasure. She was a sweet normal girl in love and I learned more of what infinite pleasure our life should hold for all of us in that week than ever surface man has for an eon.

At the week's end, my little blind witch-wife began to talk of other things than love. I will admit that I protested at length, but she gave me her reasons quietly but firmly.

"There is much you must learn, you big innocent, if you would stay alive very long down here. We may, at any time, be attacked by savage, mad ray men from the evil groups. You do not know yet how to fight or work with these tremendous weapons. We cannot wait. You have promised to do as I say for one year. My purpose was this: that I might teach you in that year to be of value to us in such a fight."

I nodded gravely, not in truth comprehending, but intrigued by the serious capable air she had suddenly put on. I did not know my Nydia.

"I shall show you the true nature of those whom you must fight tomorrow or tomorrow."

She led me to the great hall where I had first met her and paused before one of the vast machines. Her hand on the control she swung the huge distance ray projector in a long arc across the distance. Almost immediately upon the visi-screen a scene of utter horror became visible.

It was a Hell, with its Devils at work.

Do you see them, those things that should not live?"

I looked in horror upon the things that moved as men move upon the screen of life. They were a thing that could not possibly live except for the protection of the hidden caverns, and the support of the great beneficial rays keeping their degenerate and evil carcasses in motion. Small, wizened, a stench of unwashed flesh and a stench as of a slaughter house was with them. They were a kind of Goblin life, not any more human! Trolls—give them a name, they still must not live, but they do.

DEAD they must have been but for the supply of super-energy which the ancient generators poured through their bodies forever. These evil people must live on long after they would normally die—to become as undead as they were. It seems to be this fact that contributes to their evil nature, for the slow decay of their brains is energized by the synthetic electric life-force, and their resultant thought is but the reflection of life upon the stagnating brain tissues. They hung over a balcony, watching a large, white body below them that was being tortured by several similar, but larger and more brutish looking things. I can't tell you what they were doing to him, but the refinements they had for the simple job of killing a man would make Einstein envy their source of invention. He was spread out, spider-pattern, in thin strips for yards and all of it still living under the beneficial rays' miracle force. And as he shrieked, the things giggled girlishly, horribly. The pit in which they were watching the horror stunk like a glue factory, and bits of decayed flesh and blood were everywhere. The terrific augmentation of these nauseating features of the scene over the vast beam of the telaug Nydia was using made me vomit, and Nydia shut off the power.

'Now, will you learn how to fight or would you rather fall into their hands?"

"I will study diligently!" I assured my Nydia, and I meant it deeply.

"Then we will begin your education. The best way to learn to operate these terrific machines is to study the records left by those who built them. It is the way our best have learned always. The machine is called a 'dream-mech', as the right name is unpronounceable by us. The records are thought-records of the actual thought of Elder race. You will learn not directly, but indirectly, as the records are about all sorts of things, and one absorbs a knowledge of the uses and natures of the machines from the background thought of the record. So, I will start you on records we have which depict the beginning of Man on Earth, so that you may begin at the beginning, as it were. As I put different records on the 'dream-mech', you will live different lives, and when I finish, you will know more about history from little Nydia than a thousand colleges could teach you in a dozen lifetimes, for the colleges *do not* know what Nydia knows to be true of the past."

Into yet another chamber she guided me and placed me in a huge chair, like a giant's dental chair. There were several flexible metal strips which she fastened about my wrists and waist. Then she took a strange helmet fastened to a heavy cable and placed it on my head.

"Lie back and relax—you will soon be another person entirely. Don't let the sensation of being two people at once worry you, it does not last long. This is the greatest experience the wisdom of the caverns can offer you. These are the thought-records of the ancient Gods. Those which I will play for you are the records of the beginnings of life as we know it on Earth, and the records of the Messiah which we got from some Jewish ray in the mediterranean. We killed them and this record of the Messiah was among their possessions. It is a strange thing that the Gods *did* leave a Savior for men—and men killed him was true—but he was not the Christ, though Christ knew him. But enough of talk—goodbye, you are going on a long journey."

I saw her throw a Titan-size switch on the wall and in a flash a dream life more vivid than actual life by a hundred powers seized me . . .

CHAPTER II

THE RECORD OF THE BEGINNING OF MAN ON EARTH

I, DICK SHAVER—watching this mighty ruler of a planet in a place and time so far removed that mind cannot leap the gap—was like an omniscient eye belonging to a new-born God-being, one who must learn all by seeing and watching all the things that are to it unknown and mysterious.

The mind of this ruler whom I watched—this mind that was open to my eyes and to my mind as the sky—was a kaleidoscope of extremely beautiful and thrilling images of past experience. They were flowing too rapidly from the antique record for me to fully understand what this scene really was. You will more fully understand if you give your imagination full rein and do not limit it—for my words are poor tools to paint the terrific complexity of beauty and power which these thoughts of the Elder race were:

Ramon Seti III was bored. Ardala, calling on the mechanism at his side, awoke his mind somewhat and he thought slowly into the recording mech which he kept constantly running at his side: "My complaining message will have to wait. For the image of the much-desired-by-me Ardala of the Seventh Ring of Elders waits within the telaudioscreen. Her expression is alarming!"

Ardala's image became clear in the great cubical screen. She was a creature of Titanic and alien beauty. In truth she was far from what we picture by the word "human." She had peculiarities of body ungraspable by the modern mind.

She was evidently a hybrid from some other race than that of Ramon Seti III,[6] who had four limbs and, though very huge, looked much as men do today. Her three faces were nearly like our own, but her body was as if it were seen through many dividing prisms—a multiplication of rosy pale forms of feminity. Like a women seen in many mirrors, all at different angles, she had a multiplicity of charm. Like the creation of some mad genius of a cubist painter in flesh, she was beauty multiplied by additions indescribable. She was more than human, and Ramon Seti evidently held her abilities

---

[6] *Secondary thoughts of Ramon Seti III as shown by the thought record:*

I, Ramon Seti, III, have much to tell you. Though I am ruler of this city of twelve million souls, I am not happy. I would give all I possess for one day of freedom with you again, were it as it used to be when we were little shavers together.

You know how we built this city into a Nirvana, how our city is talked of throughout the Interplanetary League with envy. Now this planet city—called "Mu", by some "Terra", by others "Momoo", by still others "Erta", and by still others "Earth"—being a bit wayward in its long orbit through the dark spaces, has swung herself into the attraction of a most unpleasant sun. Within a short time she will pass so close to this sun as to heat the whole surface. Mu will become a satellite of that sun at such close proximity that men will thereafter be able to live but a thousand years, and if men still live upon the globe after the radioactive accumulations of the sun reach maximum, they will be able to stay alive but seventy years. That means the whole planet must be evacuated, and such migrations mean work. I love not work. It

in more respect than his own. She launced into a report to which Ramon listened at first with a wearied attention, then sat up, his face lighting with interest and a kind of displeasure.

"Beloved Ruler, a terrific struggle has been growing quietly and terribly from the fear of the new sun. Now it springs into full flame under our very noses. It has broken out into violence and the unbelievable fact of murder—death itself!"

"Yes, yes—my lady Elder—go on. My subjects have become so degenerate as to begin dealing death in their squabbles."

"I'll give them death!" Ramon Seti twirled his long mustaches fiercely.

"Something we did not foresee has happened to them. You who are also a student of the past will remember that when our people gave up living under any sun's light—long, long ago—the magnetic disintegrative force of the sun was well understood, was called 'de'. You will remember that 'de' was known to madden a people and cause mental aberrations, errors in the logical thought of self-interest, which avoids conflict; and under a sun's 'de' field, wars occurred among our ancestors. We had almost forgotten this detail of our far past. But now that we near Sol, the star that has attracted our loved home out of its peaceful path through dark space, and about whose deadly brightness our planet Mu will swing forevermore, the terrible 'de' has seized upon our people far more violently than ever it did in the far past, and war is now an incontrovertible fact, an evil we will not lose until we are many light years from the force fields of this sun. The rebels have seized the space-ship plants, the interplanetary landing fields and ports, and are holding them against all authority, to insure their being first to leave the planet."

"I have felt depressed myself today. Is that, too, the sun?"

"You will note, loved Lord that, the word 'depress' itself is an ancient word handed down from the times when our ancestors knew such things so well that they built the word to tell its cause. Depression is entirely due to the pressure of 'de' forces upon the mind. So the word is made up of the symbol 'de' and the word 'press'—do you understand the wisdom of our ancestors?"

"Aye, how simple of me to have not seen it myself. I remember now some of the things our teachers have told us of 'de'."

AS the ruler of all Mu planet contemplated the many-faceted beauty of Ardala and sat back satisfied with himself and all the world except for the minor troubles of a deadly approaching sun and a small revolt, outside his many chambered cavern, on the great river-wide "way of the space-hangers", the magnificent fireworks of a Titanic struggle was getting under way.

Up the broad borings and out onto the "way of the space-hangars" trundled and marched a heterogeneous army of men and machines. These were the banned men, their faces grim, intent on survival. For they had no official existence, and the chances were that when all the ships had taken off abandoning the planet to its newly acquired sun, they, not listed "officially", would be left behind. They had no wish for the fate of age which such an abandonment meant to them. They were only allowed to live their hidden existence because of the easy-going nature of Ramon Seti, who had flunked a few tests himself in his long life, and had a soft spot in his heart for those officially termed "unfit" for citizenship. Thousands of these had gradually migrated to Mu in the past centuries, for the slight and tenuous rule of Ramon Seti made life possible for them when no other metropolis would have them.

But this emergency, plus the suddenly maddening de[7] force which the sun was

---

leaves one no time for pleasure.

Every time I try to record my thoughts for you alone, old friend, I am interrupted. I am going to let our private recorder run, to show you that I have to put up with much as the ruler of all this planet city. Ruler, pah! I am the slave of twelve billion pesky people.

(Around Ramon Seti III, was all the pleasure which is a part of the life of the Atlans, and of the Titans with whom they are intermingled. The air was saturated with both nutrient vapor and beneficial vibrants, as well as with purely pleasure impulses. The nature of these vibrants is such—are synthesized electrics of a similar quality to those given off by the millions of tiny batteries that are the human body—so that it is as if the vital electric soul of woman was augmented to a million strengths and all of it sensed by the pleasure nerves of Ramon Seti's body. This is a vague idea of the Nirvana which the Titans and Atlans accepted as normal living conditions.)

[7] *Secondary thoughts upon the record of interview between Ramon Seti and Ardala, the Elder Sybyl:*

As I bend toward the cubical screen within which both the fascinating vision of the three-

pouring upon Mu, had cracked their character in that weak spot the "citizen tests" had revealed, and now, maddened and militant, they had resolved upon capturing enough of the migration ships to insure their safely leaving the doomed planet, whether anyone else did or not.

Gleaming, tremendous caterpillar tanks they had seized from the scattered slightly-guarded rodite (police) barracks, and these spearheaded their advance up the great "way of the hangers". Ahead, from the snouts of the ray weapons in the tanks, swept a vast black fan of protective rays.

Mechanical horses, painted and caparisoned like circus horses, seized from the

---

faced Ardala and the vital essence of her four-armed womanly body—I am intrigued out of my dejection by the inspiring, augmented aura and intensified inward vision accompanying the visible beauty of the wise and utterly fascinating Sybyl.

". . . my dear irresistible Ardala, you are looking positively peaked by comparison with your usual self. If I did not know it did noot exist I would say age was creeping up on you. What is the matter with you?"

"Oh, you fraud of a ruler, your inner thought is most uncomplimentary to one whom you profess to love, though I know well you are but intrigued by my unusual form and strength of character. The thing that ails me is that sun, O Lord without wisdom. The nearer we get to it, the greater is the illusion of despair, of horror, of defeat and ugliness about us engendered by the powerful field of magnetic thought-influential ionic flows about all suns. This teaching we have well-nigh forgotten since the ages when race knew a sun. Our only hope to avoid disastrous war and rioting is to begin the migration at once, and preparations have hardly begun."

"Now that you mention it, I have felt unreasonably depressed today. That is the sun? Incidentally, in spite of your objection to me as a suitor, I do love you, even today when you do not look as lovely as usual. I assure you it is not your unusual size and conformation, but the inner you which I love, for you are everything that my inner faults will not allow me to attain. Ah, Ardala, think of me differently . . ."

"It is the sun, my Lord. It has affected you, too. In weaker members of the race, it has already inflamed them to murder and madness. Mobs have taken some of the space-ship landing fields, the great space-ship factories, and are fighting over all such equipment over the whole planet. For the preparations for migration are pitifully inadequate. You should never have listened to those unwise astronomers who computed that the velocity of Erta would carry us beyond the influence of the attraction of the sun. Astronomers are notable for nothing so much as the errors of their calculations. It is known that no astronomer has ever seen a comet until it either dropped on his head or a school boy called his attention to it. Yet you have put your reputation into the hands of astronomers. It is not strange that you have lost your already worn reputation for forethought."

"What can I do, my Ardala, to retrieve the shreds of my good name? I will be reduced to a rank nearer your own, mayhap. Will you wed me then?"

"I might wed you then, you poor addle-pated bluff who has flunked every test that was ever given by the Elder wise, and got his position by his relationship to the great rulers of the Elder Planet, Hevi Enn. But you would have to become a more honest student of love than you are now. At present you are so used to being made love to that it never occurs to you to make any real efforts in that direction yourself. That attitude would have to change. I like a man who makes love to me, not one who sits and waits for me to overcome him by flattery, sensuously to arouse him so that he may supinely allow my lovemaking. No, you good looking bit of useless ornamentation for a throne, it would be a century of adversity and many a year of effort toward remaking your inner self that would shape you to my requirements in manhood. It would be easier for you to seek a less exacting mistress of your love-fate."

"Putting love iside, if I may ask your pardon for doing so, what does your superior wisdom suggest I do about the emergency which is ruining your reputation for choosing wise and able lovers? I am undone unless you can produce something in the way of advice. You must remember that in all the years I have postured as a ruler, not once has the machinery of government before required any effort on my part."

"You must take everything into your own hands, dissolve our heredity democratic rights, and devote all our energies to keeping order and to building our transportation and our passenger ships up to a sufficient number to meet the vast emergencies of moving a whole planetful of people and their belongings to a new world. Those ships we have now must begin at once the task of transferring the people to Blanocnee, the plant nearest us, which has escaped the attraction of the sun. Give orders at once, your highness; everything hinges on the next few hours. Chaos and death for most of your people if our industries' capacity for production of ships breaks down."

"You beautiful friend, you understand things so well. Suppose I appoint you my chief deputy to see that the orders you have been giving me are carried out by my people. They are somewhat unused to realizing they have a ruler. It might be better if I continue to remain in the background."

pleasure palaces, pranced side by side with the vast, waddling lizard forms of Titan-otheres, the thunder lizards, from the freight warehouses where they were used for the heavy work. The banned men, for the most part on foot, wept and screamed and fought against a light-armed and unconvincing rodite resistance.

Their goal, the great gleaming space greyhounds, waited ahead, rank on rank, in the space hangars. They were the only means on all Mu to escape the sudden and terrible dread of the sun death, of which they knew little except that it was a horrible and prolonged agony of a hideous nature.

The official citizenry, for whom the great fleet of space-ships had been assembled, heard the wildfire news of the rebellion of the banned men, and had poured out into the other ways to the hangers to fight for their right to passage in the migration ships. Less prepared and lighter-armed than the premeditated rebellion, he citizenry was more numerous, and converged on the hangers in great force, armed with light hand ray-rifles, tear-gas grenades (which were kept in every home by law), clubs and invective.

So it was that—as Ramon Seti and Ardala conducted their little tete-a-tete of mutual admiration, flirtation, and counsel—about the space-hangers was raging a riot that, to us, numerically would have been called a "war". For the Cities of the Elder races, even such nursery cities as was the Planet Mu were huge hives of life, and the tiers of endless and intricately chambred caverns contained a number of humans vast beyond comprehension.

We are used to age and accept it stoically, but to the Elder race, immortal and long free of age, it was a terrible ancient plague suddenly descending upon them, more horrible than leprosy, from which there was no escape except flight from the sun, and they did not intend to be left behind.

THE web of borings which converged on the hangars swift became a shambles of fallen men, screaming wounded wretches, trampled bodies, the huge burden "dino" beasts amuck amid it all, trampling and trumpeting terribly, the pop of the tear-gas grenades, occasionally the heavier "boom" of more deadly explosive, the sharp hiss of the dis-ray rifles picking off the guards of the hangers who were few and unprepared but fighting valiantly against all comers.

Their civilization had a horror of death, and most of the weapons used were of the immobilizing type, rays which paralyzed temporarily, sleep-gas bombs, and vibro-rays that inflicted a concussion upon the brain similar to a knock-out punch. So, scattered among the dead and dying, the maimed and the fleeing, were piles of unconsious bodies upon which the tanks rumbled, treads grinding, across which the raging mob trampled, unheeding.

And the hangars fell to the fury of the mob! A titanic tank, the driver unconscious at the controls, rumbled straight through the ranks of the rodite police, and the mob followed the swathe it had cut, straight through the crushed gates into the wide spaces where salvation lay, rank on rank, the super ships of a superior race.

And they poured aboard, the degravitors hissed and the ships floated toward the tubes, jostling each other to be first into the rock tubes that pointed at the sky. Once in, the maddened passengers threatened the attendant at the space beam apparatus till he switched on the lifter beams from fear for his life—and up and out into the voids of space and freedom from official-dom flashed the space liners, improperly manned, half-fueled, provision and equipment not even checked for the trip. These people had suddenly become less afraid of the perils of space than of official delay and red tape in the preparations for abandoning the planet.[8]

---

[8] *I would have said from watching him that Ramon Seti professed to be in love with every lovely woman he saw. But the soft and sensuous atmosphere of ultra pleasure which enwrapped the Atlan and Titan races was not one I could understand fully, even with their complex thought displayed openly before me on the thought-records. Even when I lived the very life of their minds from the great completeness of the records, I could not understand fully what they were talking about. I gathered that this mild flirtatious attitude, a simulation of deep and abiding love for each other which neither believed, was a part of etiquette, necessitated by the effect upon their thoughts and body of the extremely augmented body aura which the telepathic telesolidograph communication they used as a telephone (even when face to face). An effect which caused the mind to believe itself in love with every woman who was so augmented and so talked to in such contact. But they knew that this contact was only "love" because of the stimulative and extreme revealingness of such contacts, and so by an effort held in reserve their inner ego's freedom, which was surrendered in love only to the chosen one in love in nuptials of vastly greater augmentative awareness of the inner natures and*

RAMON SETI thought as Ardala left him alone: "This is a 'nursery' planet, all right. But it contains as well a high percentage of renegade banshees and banned "hes" from all quarters of space. But the renegades have had the grace to hide their peca-dilloes, while the new-born little men have neither grace nor the skill to conceal their shortcomings. This job is like a mother with a million separate apron strings to each of which is attached a troublesome brat.

"This sudden struggle is so profoundly unusual, I had expected anything but revolt. And after all my kindnesses to the exiled, the banned people! I knew that their de-fections would not break out unless they approached a sun. Well, now we approach a sun, and I have been so absentminded as to forget entirely that I had a large group of the banned, and that the first approach of a sun would make them stark, raving maniacs. What an ordeal it will be. I am sweating like a runner."

ACROSS the sky outside streaked the long silver roll of smoke that was the drivers of a "spacer" taking off. About the driver streaks of the exhaust were intermittent rings of gases expanding in great round flowers, which marked the notches on the accelerator as the pilot increased the drive. Ramon, glancing up, saw the streak across the sky, swung a great telaug ray to the ship, and upon the screen at his side the interior of the crowded ship sprang out in a transparent cross-section to the penetrative eye of the ray.

Ramon cursed as his eyes took in the personnel.

"Sixty per-cent maddened exiles, two per-cent just citizens. A shipload of trouble if the slightest thing goes wrong with the mechanisms of the ship. What am I supposed to do about that?"

Ramon clicked on his ship communicator, and the conductive beam he had upon the ship activated the televisor phone. The pilot lifted the lever, spoke:

"Lord Ruler, I see your face. Is it important?"

"I would advise stopping at the first space port and effecting a proper organization of your crew for emergencies in space. You are ripe for disaster. I promise you no order to detain you will go from me. Take care of those people, Pilot."

The pilot grinned.

"I would if I could, my Loved Ruler. But I have a pistol in my back and am not

---

secrets as revealed by the telepathic and vital essence augmentors.

To my observations, there was something soft and differently fibred in these immortals. Not weak, understand, but differently fibred inner makeup from our experience of character was there. Love was with them a pursuit, not a pastime. Such ways were their custom, and in the midst of a fiery revolt the ruler found time to make love to the lady who brought him the information of his people's peril for the first time. Just what was the outcome of this affair between the ruler and the Elder Lady of the many facets, I never learned; for her vital image faded from the screen, herself in more awareness of the need for haste and action in the emergency.

It was evident to the mind that to Ramon Seti a revolt was a nothing, a thing that could not be serious, a thing that had never happened before and could not happen now, a thing to throw to a lady to handle because she was more interested in it than any one else. Such lazy thought habits had become ingrown in them; there was an absence of awareness of how cruel and violent Nature can be when she drives men to war.

For their race had evolved an endless wealth of life-supporting machinery, due to the infinite capacity of work enjoyed by their immortal scientists. The true necessity for hard labor had long left their race. They were the richer for it, but to my way of seeing, they needed conflict with something to harden them, to tune them to full efficiency. Evidently their approach to our Sol was giving it to them.

They had a saying: "Work is something a fool must endure because he cannot think of a way to accomplish his purpose without it." If you could see—had seen—their mechanisms you would understand what they meant and know it for a true saying.

But the necessity for real and swift labor had arisen because of their suddenly discovered susceptibility to the detrimental and maddening energies of the rapidly approaching sun. They had to leave this planet, this drifting hunk of rock called Mu, much sooner than they had planned upon because they might not approach as near the sun as they thought. Their bodies could stand it but their minds could not! (Though the fact that some of them did approach the sun and live under it for an age is well known. But they did not do so because they wanted to do so.)

in command. "Perhaps when we leave the sun[9] behind they will cool off and I can manage proper precautions. Is that all, Sire?"

"Good luck, Pilot. That's all."

IN spite of all the Atlan care to avoid bloodshed, many died as the war went into its short climax.

Ramon Seti sent his autographed message that safety and transportation to the new world would be guaranteed every one, no matter what their status—if they lay down their arms.

But they were fear stricken, an emotion long unknown among the men of these races. They would not give up the ship ports. Steadily the degravitor rays hissed upward through the rock launching tubes that led to the sky far above, the sky that had always been dark, but now was lit by the deadly unwanted light of the sun.

As the rays, which were a reversed flow of gravity-causing ions, flicked on, another great space ship roared its jets upward into the heavens.

The rebels had no way of knowing the fate of these vessels whether captured by Atlan vessels once out in space or not. But flee the Sun they would and did. Half the ships were gone with but half the potential passenger capacity filled before they finally dropped the last banned man in sleep beside his heated shorter generator, with his paralysis wave variator device in his hand beside him. (This was a long crook-like handle, which, inserted in certain beam generators, made an atunement possible which gave off a beam of a nature similar to the energy impulses of the nerves of the body, and this energy was distorted in vortices as it is in epilepsy). It was a less harmless weapon than the sleep beam, as its use could be adapted to many harmless beam generators to make them into weapons.

The migration took place, but meanwhile a group of leading scientists came to realize that they knew very little of the effects of sun energies upon life—of the effects of disintegrant energies and magnetic flows from suns upon the human animal's brain and nervous system, and decided to do something about it.

Once this ignorance had not been the case, for the original men who were the source of the Atlan and Titan races had been the sun-planet dwellers and used to all the horrors of sun-bathed life. But they had conquered the mysteries of their age and their wars had finally been understood. They learned finally that only in dark space on a cold sphere far from any sun could life exist without the phenomena of war and age taking their over-toll of the best things in life.

It was those original mighty thinkers who had pioneered the first voyage into space. It was the men who followed in their footsteps who pioneered the living methods that made life possible within the warm undershells of the cold planets of dark space. And it was then they learned that age did not come to a man why stayed far enough away from a sun—but only greater and greater youth and growth, only a greater flame of life as age made him stronger instead of weaker as near a sun.

It was this Titanic growth force of life without the braking disintegrance of a

---

[9] *At first approach of the Earth to the sun, it came quite close to the terrible heat of the sun. The flames of the sun scoured Earth clean of all the God-race work, the whole surface became a great flame and flows of lava ran like rivers, sealed most of the great openings into the depths. The heat was of short duration. The Earth swung on out into the cold again, eventually taking up her present orbit around the sun. But in the deep caverns lived the only survivors of the heat, our ancestors—or did anyone live?*

Did our ancestors come later? Long after Earth had known the God-race, did some space ship of wanderers return at last from space and settle once again on Mother Earth—or will we ever know?

But the broad implications of the Genesis of the bible would seem to lend themselves to support this legend of the cavern people—that Adam and Eve were an experiment in the effects of "de" upon the race of Elder people, and that we are the result of that experiment. It would seem rather logical, if we are their children or even their pet animals—or even their slave race—that they would thus leave an atmosphere they know to be so evil in its effects— here could be one explanation—they wanted to see what the effects would be. Did they find out? Is that the reason they are never seen on earth anymore? Somehow, it seems to me that the people who most deserved it have been "elevated" many times from earth, as in the legend the Norse tell of their winged maidens taking up the bravest warriors to Valhalla. There are many such legends—as the legend of Jesus Christ being taken up to heaven. There are scores of them. One finds it as easy to believe all of these legends as to select any particular one for belief. The belief in the underworld is the most persistent, for a good reason— it still exists, and is still a wonderland, and still a hell of weird conflict and lost hope for all men.

sun that built up the vast formidable civilization which was the Atlan and Titan fabric. This was the fabric of the city planets, and their ruling, leading Elder God planets where those who survived all the few dangers of their life had to go eventually because of their ever increasing size. Their undying nature had given them immortal life, but it had also given them the problem of ever-increasing size to worry about. They conquered this problem by moving on to ever larger and larger planets, and the slightly increasing gravity of each made them able gradually to accustom their growing bodies to the increasing gravity.

Too, they had "adjusted gravity" rooms, where the upward speeding particles of magnetic flows similar in content to the downward push of gravity made their weight slight, even upon a heavy planet to which they would have been unable to adjust themselves ordinarily.

So it was that the beautiful, four-armed, three-faced Sybyl of strange race, with the many-faceted feminine body which was Ramon's unattainable desire, called the good-natured ruler and informed him that the rebellion of the banned men had been put down at last, and that the city was under martial law and would remain so.

As Nydia and I watched the ancient records, the illusion was perfect from the magnificent antique mechanism. We were actually present, time had been set back and we lived again the life that was when life was perfection on earth. But it is impossible fully to describe such records to you. They are full of a mighty thought symbol, a conceptual richness of which we can form but the slightest echoes of the true and full meaning.

And as another jam-packed ship would flash skyward, the assembled, futilely struggling, immovably jammed citizenry below would groan loudly in unison, for each upward streaking grey shape meant another avenue to safety from the sun had been cut off. Rebels and citizenry were now inextricably mingled, and manned the ships as soon as the tubes emptied—crammed themselves into the mighty spacers and roared off, for an immense acceleration is possible within the sky-pointing rock tunnels when the degravitors within the tubes countered the down-pull of gravity with an uprushing flow of ions, making the ship as weightless as it would be in space.

All this sudden struggle was profoundly unusual among the people of Mu (Earth), every one was unusually and intensely excited—minute by minute television broadcasts went over the whole planet describing the contestants down to the lowliest electric truck driver engaged. No one in truth took it very seriously, for a bloody war's realities of madness and universal death was to them an "idea", a "reaction" for which their brains were unprepared by past occurrence. It just couldn't "happen", but it *was* happening before their eyes.

Half of their precious ships for the migration were gone or destroyed in the struggle before the last maddened rebel dropped in sleep beside his heated ray generator, his paralyzing nerve-ray rifle empty of energy in his hands.

You have just read the first 20,000 words of Richard S. Shaver's tremendous "Thought Record" novel of the life of Christ as obtained by him by telaug from the people of the caves. In all, this novel is 200,000 words long, and will not be published in any other magazine. Don't miss the opportunity to read all of this thought-provoking novel. Keep up your membership! Next issue within two months.

—The Editor

HEIREN'S FRIEND,
George Murman

By Richard S. Shaver

THOUGHT for today: "Almost all criminals have some such character as George Murman in their heads."

Psychiatrist examining William Heirens: "Why bother assuming any other reality than the universal desire to have another assume their guilt?"

Why bother!

Here are some more of the utterances of these extremely thorough workers in the vineyard!

From the Press accounts of the Heirens trial, taken from my scrap book of clippings:

"Among local experts who identified Murman was Dr. David B. Rotman, director of Psychiatric Institute of the Municipal court.

"Heirens friend Murman" he said "was none other than the mythical companion in crime referred to by countless law violators I have interviewed.

"Caught with the goods, these fellows all tell you that 'George did it'." Dr. Rotman explained.

Dr. Rotman then went on to say: "If Heirens has a split personality, there is no evidence of it in his statement or behavior."

"Heirens has given no indication of living an unnatural fantasy life—not even been suspicious of food . . ."

The newspaper reporter then says: "One authority, supplementing Dr. Rotman's listing of schizoid characteristics, pointed out that among other important traits are inability to concentrate and to plan and carry things through."

"But" (the authority says) "Heirens planned a series of burglaries, and his success in his studies shows the reverse of this condition . . ."

End of press quotes.

I must ask these authorities this: If, as you say, Heirens was not bugs, was not addicted to fantasy, was only manufacturing an alibi, and had good marks in his studies —WHY WASN'T HE INTELLIGENT ENOUGH TO KNOW THAT A GEORGE MURMAN LIVING INSIDE HIM WOULD DO HIM NO GOOD AS AN ALIBI?

This is the point where "authorities" usually fall down in their explanations of these phenoma we have come to call the Shaver mystery.

It is rather evident that Heirens knew better than to commit the crimes he did, and that he knew better than to try to fake an alibi which entailed official acceptance of a character named George Murman who "lived inside him". Yet he told that tale, and he committed those crimes attributed to him.

Could it be that Heirens was intelligent enough to know his goose was cooked anyway, he might as well tell the truth, it didn't matter what he said? It wasn't even worth inventing lies to cover up his undeniably weird inhabitant.

But, in spite of the "authorities" who explain away all such phenomena with their matter-of-fact words that mean so little, there *are* George Murmans, who *can* control people from a distance, with invisible rays, make it appear that they "live inside one"—"which countless law violators refer to when caught".

Rotman has heard "countless" such stories as Heirens by his own words, and must know that there is vastly more to such stories than "George did it" alibis. (Or does he secretly think it is "spirits"—avoid that for fear of ridicule? Or is he one who ges the forbidden fruit of stim rays, and considers it a form of payment for his official scepticism when faced with a George Murman? Or are all officials singularly ungifted with deductive powers, and can never sense the truth of such allegations as Heirens of George Murman's presence?)

The real truth is that knowledge of the rays and their source is rather general. It is known, talked of among those who know, and officially it is frowned upon for reasons rather numerous.

First, there is the reason of danger. They fear that George Murman against whom they have no modern defense or any other kind, may descend upon them if they countenance the truth of his existence.

Second there is fear of ridicule from those who do not know that such things exist in spite of public scepticism.

Thirdly there is the economic fear that the scepticism, coupled with the machinations of a character that delights in murdering little girls with an Heirens, will delight in causing their loss of job or worse, deviling them to death, unseen and untouched, if they so much as mention the possibility of his existence.

Fourth, there is the mighty obstacle that clinches the problem: it is incredible to the modern educated man that anything of the kind could exist, because he has so rigorously been taught that "it is incredible".

But if any man of normal deductive powers had all those "countless" stories from the mouths of criminals and others which Rotman had to investigate, he would come inevitably to the inescapable conclusion, just as Rap did when confronted with it—that there was "something" not generally understood, something unseen but very much existent, SOMETHING more than imagination behind these stories.

For they are extremely TOO "countless", too incredibly prevalent and simultaneous in their coincident corroboration each of the other, these stories. TOO, TOO "countless" are these weird parallels in these stories of George Murman and his likewise invisible counterparts.

Inescapably these gentlemen in Dr. Rotman's position are forced into these repetitive explanations of the unexplainable.

If you readers whose interest has caused you to read this far are really interested in the George Murmans who cause crimes and may one day take hold of you, too, and make a murderer or worse out of you—you too will keep a notebook and in it paste all such press accounts of the confessions of the William Heirens of the world.

Note for yourselves, without such pointing out as here indulged in, the "countless" times that unexplainable incidents occur just as some tragedy results from these same incidents.

For instance, the train wreck reported in *Life Magazine* with pictures, recently: the brakemen, looking out along the side of the front train (of two-part flyer) noted what he "thought was a brake shoe flying off. He quickly stopped the train, ran back to investigate. As he returned, after finding "nothing wrong", the second part of the train crashed into the rear of the coaches at some ninety miles an hour.

A trivial incident caused a lot of deaths, an incident so trivial as to be almost lost in the account of the misery and pain and excoriation of the system that caused the wreck.

Yet a simple little projection with a mechanism known to many people on the surface could cause the picture of a brake shoe flying off to make a brakeman stop a train. In fact, such a projection *did* cause that wreck, and many officials know it, but cannot say it for fear of ridicule and loss of their job or worse. For it is "incredible" that machines exist that are not known to the "scientific" world, although it is distinctly not incredible to those who have seen and experienced the working of these machines.

Notice a few of these incidents, and help us expose once and for all the existence of the secret groups responsible for these wrecks.

Officers of the law know a great deal about George Murman, they meet up with him frequently. But they cannot officially countenance the existence of invisible forces, no matter how visible they become, no matter how many little Degnans they kill. Because they would lose their jobs or wind up in the nuthouse. Nevertheless there is so much inescapable evidence that their often fine deductive minds cannot always refuse to mention the existence of such things. So greatly is this true that the newspapers almost invariably catch an echo of this invisible George Murman and his terrific influence on crime—and almost invariably this unseen echo creeps into news accounts of crimes like Heirens'. In Heirens case, where the criminal was young enough and smart enough to know it (or think) didn't matter whether he told about Murmans or not, it came in with a loud hurrah, and everyone knows there was a George Murman who lived inside Heirens. Whenever these particular crimes and criminals are carefully reported, this invisible creature is seen and heard from the mouths of men like Heirens who have given up hope of life, and see no reason for concealing the exact truth of their experiences. Like Heirens they do not expect to be believed, they just get tired of lying and so tell the truth—and it gets into the news.

Many of such students of the criminal mind have noted this coincidence of the invisible companion, just as did Dr. Rotman, "countless" times. And invariably, like Dr. Rotman, they "explain" it away in the most readily accepted way, as the universal desire to find a scapegoat, an alibi. BUT every Dr. Rotman, if we got down to the bottom of their mind, beneath the shield they have erected between their knowledge of the truth and the public attitude toward this truth, would admit that there are invisible forces, voices they hear quite as often as did poor Heirens, things not explainable according to accepted dictates of medicine, things that ordinary common "sense" cannot accept. You would find these men surreptitiously investigating "spiritualism", buying expensive apparatus for the detection of hidden radios, and similar activities to get to the bottom of the cause of the phenomena so clearly brought out by Heirens' confession. They know that George Murman is not a figment of Heirens' imagination, but they cannot publicly admit such a belief, for they would forfeit the respect of men who do not know the evidence that their mind cannot explain away as easily as their words explain it all away as "alibi". No criminal with the sense to act as Heirens acted during his trial, with the cunning to be believed in telling a tale as wild as an invisible being which made him act as he acted. He only told that story because it was the exact truth.

To students of the Shaver Mystery, the case of Heirens is a type case, a case that shows the terrible evil that afflicts men everywhere, and has for centuries lied and concealed itself behind a facade of misunderstanding and official fear of ridicule.

There are *many* George Murmans, and they do inflict terrific damage on mankind. For the dero invariably attack our best and most lovable and most capable people. The George Heirens case, in this view, is *NOT* typical. If Heirens had been an embryo scientist, it would have been typical. Frank's case—"Leopold and Loeb", remember!—that was typical, yet nothing was said of invisible influences that I remember.

Clarence Darrow was too clever a man to let the "ghost" creep into his defense. There was no method of proof of such a condition influencing the minds of his clients, Loeb and Leopold. So Darrow did not use it. But if we knew the truth, we would find some strange things in the lives of Loeb and Leopold, things that only readers of *Weird Tales* ever enjoy reading.

For these rays and the mad members of the life of the Elder world of caverns do exist, and do inflict men with the terrible crimes and mental tamper that result in such things as the Frank murder, and as the Degnan murder.

Over the Rocky mountains are areas that planes habitually avoid. Not because of height, no, because something causes wrecks, something makes the instruments lie—and they crash into mountains.

Many pilots cannot avoid these areas, because the non-superstitious plotters of transcontinental flights cannot see any reason in going out of a straight line for superstitions vague warning. So we have continual wrecks such as the one that took the life of Carole Lombard and sixteen army officers on a flight to California. We read of these wrecks continually in the papers. Does it never occur to anyone that there are too many of them to account for by natural causes. Yes, it does, but what else can they blame?

Then there are the cases like Mrs. Shirley Vetter of Seattle. She and her husband were honeymooning when she fell striking her head on a rock. She says:

"It didn't hurt much. I got up but when I had taken a few steps, I *suddenly* felt a *terrific pain,* in my head, and fell into the water."

Mrs. Vetter, the clipping goes on to say, was blind nearly a year. Mysteriously, during the birth of a baby her sight returned. For the first time in a year, she saw, the first sight she saw was her day old baby!

Very odd coincidences, but if you are a clipping collector, not odd at all. They are usual in these accounts.

It interprets, to one in the know, like this: When you hurt yourself, it furnishes an alibi for a fiend with a ray. He can hurt you then, and even his "people" who understand cannot be sure it was a ray injury or an actual injury. So he blinds the young woman because he is an inverted sadist, and takes pleasure in hurting women. A psychologist will tell you that what a sadist wants to hurt is what a normal man would admire. His "love" is the equivalent of a normal man's hate, his "hate" a normal man's love.

Now the woman, blind, is noticed by the "white" ray, or white witchcraft, and these people are guilty of frequently causing medical "miracles", making cripples walk, blind to see. But they too are under the injunction to keep their presence hidden. They must wait an opportunity so that their act is not noticed, too. They have a natural sympathy for a woman in childbirth, and want to help her, often do help childbirth. It is a simple matter for them to play a healing ray along the woman's eye nerves and repair the damage done by the sadist ray a year before. This is news hidden from us by these "crime-proof" reporters, who cannot ever admit that there is not any explanation but the actual of invisible forces, for these "miracles," which have been explained by reporters in more ways than any thaumaturgist could ever think of using.

Summing up—if you really want to know the truth, keep clippings, and use your deductive powers. There is endless evidence.

DO EVERYTHING YOU CAN, TODAY

By RICHARD S. SHAVER

* * *

SHE had watched all night the screen. Now he got up out of bed, up there so many thousand feet above her, and she went on watching to keep burning the plea-fire of writing he was doing. For men and earth needed nothing so much as to know their enemy and struggle against the dark hidden throttling of his culture, of his freedom, of his mind that was going on.

"Do everything you can today."

She had watched over him for twelve years, keeping off the needle rays of the mad dero, and had never before said that to him. Now she said it, and he heard and thought of the years that such as her had watched over him keeping off the needle rays of the dero, cutting, cutting at his mind. Keeping off the death that threatened not only himself, but the whole race of man. How many dero, how few sane people trying for the future? Up here on the surface, too, how many casual fritterers of time, how many criminal destroyers of liberty and safety and culture? How many war-mongers, how many panderers, how many seducing man into another thing than man, into a slothful resistless creature that let his life be consumed by an enemy race, an enemy alien and evil?

He sat down at the battered typewriter, wrote this. It was not good, no more could his mind flame at the barriers like a giant of strength, like a master of cunning forming the words so that no man could resist them. Only could he repeat the truth, over and over—there is an unseen and terrible enemy destroying, robbing, denying man all the things that life could be without them. They are not even mentioned by other writers. They must be understood. We must know our friends among the cavern people, and we must care for the little they can give us from the Elder culture, not look upon their message as spook talk, or angel hand-waving, or any other foolish thing, we must know and see the truth of those who work for us night and day in the darkness, risking more than we risk and suffering more than we suffer, and having more than we have to lose. We must know these friends and do what we can for their work, for them, and for ourselves. The darkness has been in our minds too, too long, we have wondered about the unseen too ignorantly, too incredulously, too stupidly ignored all their effort. We have been stupid about the voices, about the visions and dreams, and that day must pass when we fear the people of the caverns. That day must pass when they countenance our destruction and the obstacles the mad dero among the caves raise against our science must be removed. We can help, and we must. Only could he write it over and over, and wonder when he would be understood. Wonder when the Boff Perrys and Kennedys of fandom would know that Shaver was not just a fool writer, but was a man bringing a new and great thing into life and into science fiction—the discovery of the caverns and their Elder science. The horizons of yesterday were being destroyed, and the super-science stfandom worshipped as the future would be seen by all of them to be the past, a concrete terrific vital living science that could be resurrected from the remnants still waiting for man in the caverns and now being stolen by the aliens from space. Stolen while our own native hobs and secretive, scurrying, hiding, gibbering native life of the caverns let it be stolen for want of understanding how to do differently. For that custom of secrecy that had guarded the cavern mech until man had grown able to study and benefit by its science was now operating to defeat all men, to defeat the purpose for which it had been begun. Letting in the alien life of space through the caves where Earth's heritage could be stolen without man even knowing he had possessed the Gods' best gift.

VOICES IN THE NIGHT
By RICHARD S. SHAVER

KELLY was down here. The toughest mayor in town." I am asked: "Why don't you tell the newspapers about this?"

A lot of people ask me that in their letters. "Why don't you tell the newspapers, or the F.B.I., or Congress?"

Truth is I'd love to, and it is a patriotic duty, BUT . . .

Other nations are down there, Yugo-Slavia, Ex-Nazis, French, English (though not "official" English) Portuguese. They are all hard at work, moving out the wonder-mech to caverns under their own country, and laughing up their sleeves at the "Modern" Americans, who are so modern they cannot believe in the Elder races. There are Mongols from under Tibet, strangers from the ends of earth, and they all know very well why Shaver does not tell his country about the caverns and their wealth which his country is losing by its short-sighted incredulity.

They *could* go down there, our native American people *could* also benefit from the ancient mechanisms, but there is, apparently, no way to tell a newspaper editor that Witchcraft is still news today. Being raised in the modern school of thought that does not believe in anything but the "General Motors" form of omniscience, the American secret agent *discounts all* that is *not easily understood, never* reports anything of the disturbing nature covered by Shaver writings.

There are plenty of people down there, hoping and praying that someone like Shaver *does* break through the dense cloud of "modern" ignorance in America and get some *action* out of our powerful nation before less worthy rulers than our own Republicans and Democrats take over, both up and down. They would like to forget what they are going through in their battle with the dero of the caverns, they would like someone else to help with that battle. Bu they find no way of telling the U.S. that will be believed and acted upon. There *is* no greater ignorance than the blindness engendered by the sense of all-knowing self-sufficient ignoramus-ego consciousness which our educational fol-de-rol has given our average American public school product.

Voices in the night say: "Tell 'em outright, get 'em down here, we need 'em plenty!" How I wish I could, I *love* those people fighting for us down there and ignored by our "omniscient" statesmen, so much wiser than the "crack-pots" of the world, who keep writing them "crank" letters. It might be wise to afflict some of these infinitely wise dunderheads with a plague of Underwoods and Woodstocks, enough clever letters to the right genelemen might bring about an investigation of the possibility of the Elder Caverns. It might also bring about a suppression of Shaver, who knows? You oppositional stf fans, (numbering all of one hundred) take note. It might work!

Other ways to work: Watch that little guy you noticed, find out where he goes, what he is up to. Silly? Sure, but they do come up for things, and they are dero. Quite often.

Under other nations, certain gentlemen found a way to collect on the knowledge of the caverns. Naturally they would like to sell to the U.S. too, maps of entrances, nature of mech and valuables to be found, maps of the cavern layout. But they, no more than I, can find a way to penetrate the thick skull of the "educated" American official. Less "well-cultured" countries, Turkey, Russia, Iran *buy* these products from the cavern people, go down and bring them up, go back down after more, are working and getting somewhere. But not the official U.S. government, not they. They're too smart to be taken in by any such "hoax". They don't hear voices, no matter how many voices they hear.

"Tell 'em, but right!" the voice says. I am to believe the worthy psychiatrists that it is an illusion, with thousands of letters from thousands of fans, of people who hear voices, similar voices to my own, to back me up in my illusions. I am to believe that my own excursion to the underworld was also imaginary. I am to believe I am a "crackpot" even when I look in ancient writings and find the same illusions in many writers, taken quite seriously, those men of the past. But they were taken seriously when they spoke of winged horses, too. Some of the letters I get are about that wild, too. Sometimes I wonder if crackpots are crazy, and the worthy know-it-all is not so wrong. These thousands of letters are all from crack-pots who have simultaneous illusions then? These voices are all imaginary? Every voice, every sight is a vision. The evidence of the senses cannot be trusted when the pedants say: "It is not so!"

The only trouble is I know better, and they don't. I have scars, and they don't. I have seen and know, and they don't. They only have ears which they do not use. They have only "deductive?" senses which are to deduce and reconstruct the truth from what they hear. They cannot do this for they do not know.

I would like to accept their comforting view that "voices are illusion", that the caverns and the deros are also "imaginary", due to a fevered, cracked brain, that three airplanes disappearing in today's headlines, containing fourteen men in the crews, and the steady succession of accidents and wrecks and catastrophes and fires are all all "accidents" in truth, that there are no "deros", even though I have felt their searing rays, have been tormented, pursued. Naturally it would be comforting to assume I am suffering from a convenient "persecution complex" and forget about it. Naturally it is presumptuous to assume I know about something the Government itself does not know about. All these people who write are of course also suffering from the same sort of ailment.

Only trouble is I know that every person that ever tried to tell a government anything was afflicted with the same timid assumption that no person could know something that a government did not.

The first prospector ever to find an oil field must have had the same thought: "How is it that I know this, and the mighty U.S. government does not know it?"

But there is also a first time for everything, and this is one of them. Peculiarly, though, it is not a first. Many, many have written their "crank" letters to government officials, many other people have tried to enlighten the "science" of the world as to the existence of the Elder caves. I am not the first.

Here's hoping they do wise up, and get in there. There exist in the caves weather machines, set in a vast network all over the country, that can control the precipitation, the winds, the whole character of the weather. I know it, have seen it, how do I tell ANYONE?

These millions of tons of infinitely valuable machinery are today being culled over by engineers from several other countries and the best of it shipped off to the other side of the world. The best of it!

The finest of it has already been shipped off to space, bit by bit, for centuries. But there remains all the heavier installations, too great for even the powerful drives of the Elder ships to take away. These are trundling toward Iran, toward the Kremlin, toward Tibet, toward Sweden underground!

How can truth assume so incredible, so unconveyable, so utterly unacceptable a form. Is this me, sane and safe and practical me, saying these things to people? I guess it is and may the Gods help me do it right!

Gypsies know about the underworld. Hex doctors know. Spiritualists do not. The spiritualist is "enlightened", the hex doctor is "superstitious".

Did YOU ever ask a weather man what became of the rain that started raining and suddenly quit—against all probability? Did you ever ask a prison guard how come certain guards shot and killed certain other guards? Did YOU ever ask the missing persons bureaus of cities where the missing people went. Did you ever talk to the insurance gentlemen who ascertain the cause of fires, the nature of the mechanical failures in train wrecks—all the many things that unaccountably go wrong?

No, but you KNOW there was nothing mysterious about it all! How do you KNOW it? You assume it, because of the nature of your education.

All I can say is hurrah for the witch doctors! They know something is true of the dark things that happen in life. They don't close their eyes to all the unseen things of life. But a modern "professor" *can* so close his eyes (and does).

Brewster had nothing on the gentlemen who profit from the "secrecy" about the caves. No income tax, and secret weapons by the million, and a "police force" who call them "superstition". Hurrah for superstition, say they.

Yet, truth is, they often *wish* for the good old U.S. army when a swarm of wild dero show up from some unobserved source attack, and they find the weapons they had considered invincible are equaled by the weapons the wild dero inherited from their forefathers.

But if they live through it, they call it "over", and go on ducking the income tax.

How to tell American citizens of this throttling commercial strangle hold the unseen cavern profiteers have on them, how to tell it and be believed.

How to tell the American government that there is something to learn about the rocks of mother Earth. How? It is only Shaver rattling his crack-pot. Throw it in the basket.

How to tell labor of the slave labor sweat shops of the caverns? How to tell anyone anything they do not already know? How is it done?

How to tell people there are capitalists who *fit* the awful pictures drawn of them in Russian cartoons. As easy as to tell a Russian the cartoons capitalist papers carry of communists are true pictures.

But both are right in some instances, wrong in others. There are good and bad rulers in the caves, good and bad "sweat shop" operators, some feed the workers enough, and give them a day off once a week. Others neither feed them, nor pay them, nor give them any days off.

And I shouldn't have bothered saying it because it would never be accepted by the staff of an American college as sanity.

I shouldn't have exerted myself in the face of the egregious incredulity of the average man—I just shouldn't bother. Let the monopoly roll on, it will anyway. I would like to talk to just one F.B.I. agent, and see what he knows about it all—one of those gentlemen who has all the "information" about everything in his files. I'd like to know just what THEY *are* doing, those incredibly healthy users of the ancient stim mech ben.

Do you think I'd learn? Do you think any of those worthy agents of practical-wisdom's-indication-to-action would have a word to to say about the unavoidable evidences of underworld activity, of Shaver's "dero" destruction? Do you think I'd get anything out of them but silence? Shamefacedly they *might* admit there was something "strange" going on, and that is all! Yet any moron can put the picture together out of a few cases like Heirens' tale of George Murman. Do you think all our criminal investigation is so blind as not to know there really are George Murman influences? Of course they know. Like Shaver, they don't know *how* to talk about it without being looked at askance. And don't think I don't worry about being so bold as to mention it. Every time the neighbors look at me, I suspect they have read some thing I have written and decided I was "nuts". Yes, I have that much sense! I worry about these things the same way you do, and more often! I *know* it is an impossible job to tell about the dero but I know it is the *most necessary work,* because I *know what* they *do!* So did Heirens know! So should *you,* to keep you from becoming an Heirens! So should the F.B.I. know! Because they *do* know, they have nothing to say to these incredibly "ignorant" ravings by Shaver.

"By DuPont". Think about that! *Did* all the technological processes "discovered" by Dupont research come from their laboratories? Did not *some* of them come from the records still to be found in sealed record containers in the caverns. If DuPont *knew* of this terribly valuable source of commercial techniques, of manufacturing secrets learned by a million years of culture by a greater race—*would* HE *TELL YOU* ABOUT IT? Yet people write me letters asking me: "Why does this secrecy about the caverns exist?" Dupont laboratories could tell you about it, if they wanted to. But that wouldn't be good business, would it?

There are other such secret groups. The DuPonts—if they are included—are not alone. And I had to say *if,* I couldn't assume that DuPont knew! That would be incredible, wouldn't it? But isn't it *odd* that the "modern" age progressed so rapidly when so *many* centuries went by while men developed so little beyond a better set of harness for the horses? Or did they develop that? Maybe the Egyptians' harness was better! Some of the tomb drawings include pictures of telaugs labeled by our egyptologists "mysterious" picturizations of "unexplained mechanical contrivances".

LETTERS FROM READERS

Dear Mr. Geier:

While in California in August of last year, my husband and I called on Mr. Edward Johns of San Francisco. We found Mr. Johns very communicative, and here is the gist of what we learned.

1. Mr. Johns claims to have talked often with beings of another dimension but didn't say if he received any information or much else. Claims they looked like full sized versions of fairies. Upon approaching them too closely you automatically were snapped into their dimension and couldn't get back. This happened in Mendocino County, Cal.

2. Mr. Johns claims that these forces rampant in Mendocino county have tried to get him to lay off, and he told us that he was trying to negotiate with them for a large sum of money in exchange for his silence.

3. Mr. Johns claims that he and a teacher from Stanford University have located a gadget buried in Mendocino county, and when we visited him, he was building some sort of apparatus to nullify the force emanating from it. He believed it to be some sort of machine that affected one's thoughts, because he and this teacher dug for over half a day and excavated a hole only a couple of feet wide and about six to twelve inches deep. They are both fairly strong men and the effort involved in digging this "hole" left them both very much exhausted.

4. Mr. Johns claims to know two men whom he says are from other worlds, and which are at present involved in a struggle to see who will dominate the Earth. One of these men—whom he sees often—has a large hole in his throat which in a normal man would be fatal. This man is able to get a terrific wattage output from a radio circuit while the tubes are cold.

5. Mr. Johns said that once for two weeks he was taken aboard a space ship and given training and that one day while piloting the space ship he suddenly discovered he was about to crash into an astral body of some sort. It was too late to avoid it so he drew all the power the ship was capable of and as it touched the body he turned on a beam or something, and the body was exploded into nothing. He says that shortly afterward he saw in a San Francisco newspaper an article telling about astronomers seeing a star explode for some unknown reason.

All this was told us by Mr. Johns, and we have only his word for it. He also mentioned an area in Maine which has no towns or villages of any sort for several hundred square miles. While we were at his home we got out a map and checked, and this region definitely exists. Mr. Johns heard about it from an army man who arrived in S.F. about the same time we did. This army officer insisted men had gone into this region and disappeared and others have come out completely mad. Why, nobody seems to know . . . Cecelia Mollett, 510 Haynes Street, Dayton, Ohio.

* * *

Dear Mr. Geier:

I am very much interested in the Shaver Mystery and perhaps I can forward a bit of information to you that might prove interesting. Last summer my brother and I went on a long expedition into the woods for the purpose of finding caves that might prove interesting. One evening as we were making camp, just about the time the sun began to set, I noticed that the woods were extraordinarily quiet. It was not the quietness of night, for not even the sounds of night birds and animals, or even bugs, were evident. We had scarcely retired when we suddenly heard the most-chilling screech I have ever heard in my life. Suffice it to say, that though we investigated, we found nothing. Even during the following day we found no trace of any wild life whatsoever. Even the foliage around us had a peculiar "dead" appearance. Also, there was no wind or breeze in the vicinity at all. For those interested, the area mentioned is in Bear Mountain Interstate Park, and is approximately three miles north of Lake Tiorati, and a little west along the R.D. trail. Perhaps this area might be worth investigating. Unfortunately my brother and I didn't have time . . . Oliver J. Barton, Jr., 13 Irving Place, Summit, N.J.

* * *

Dear Mr. Geier:

Not too long ago a person who gave his name and address as Thomas Andrews, Hotel Pierre, N.Y.C., wrote a letter to the Discussions dept. of AMAZING STORIES, in which he claimed to have seen what he thought was a space ship, while on a hunting trip in the Pokono Mountains of Pennsylvania. He extended an invitation to anyone who wished to accompany him, on a return trip to the spot, this coming summer.

I decided to see him about it and so, went to the Hotel Pierre and asked for his room number. I was told that no one by that name had registered within the past six months—or had a future reservation. Through my office, (I'm a private investigator) I checked up on every Thomas Andrews in N.Y.C. proper, and all denied having written the pre-stated letter. (There were some thirty odd in all.)

I tell you this for what it is worth, feeling that all cranks should be exposed if anything constructive is to be done . . . Arnold J. Lipman, 1630 Macombs Road, Bronx, N.Y.

* * *

Dear Mr. Geier:

I'm glad to see that someone is doing something to start some organized research on the "Shaver Mystery." No open-minded person can help but be interested in it as there are too many phases of the mystery that stir up vague memories in everyone's mind. For example, about four years ago a friend and I were exploring a small cave near our homes in Pittsburgh, Pa. It seemed to end, but we discovered a round tube near the floor. It was almost filled with sand at the entrance, but when we dug some away the rest was clear, and we proceeded through the foot-and-a-half tube, with our Scottie dog in the lead. We were about one hundred feet in the tunnel, which sloped at a twenty or so degree angle when we heard a very deep sound. It was not loud, and seemed to be felt more than heard. The dog was out of sight ahead, but not for long. He let out a screech—which is the only way I can describe it—and raced back over us, clawing as he went. We got out as quickly as we could and couldn't find our dog. He had never run away like that before, no matter what the circumstances, but this time he was gone. We finally found him at home, acting queerly, and he wouldn't go near any of us for quite some time. We didn't return to the cave for quite some time, and when we finally did, armed with rifles, we found that the whole cliff had been dynamited by the railroad company, and the entrance to the cave was buried under tons of rock and ground. There are also records of a robber band who used to disappear in that vicinity after raids on the surrounding towns. The trail led to the plateau atop the cliffs, and though the area was thoroughly searched and guarded for months, no signs of a cave was ever found. Yet, one of the gang was killed, and before he died, he mentioned something about an "automatic door," but that was all. I don't know how much more information we can get on this, but we'll try . . . Lyon McCandless Jr., U.S.N.R., Cecil Field, Jacksonville, Fla.

* * *

Dear Mr. Geier:

A few days ago I was out rabbit hunting in the hills south of my home. I was walking alone, looking at a hill in front of me that appeared to have a cave of some sort at the base of it. As I neared it I found the bodies of four dead puppy coyotes. I don't know however, if I can definitely link up these dead bodies with what I found in the cave next to them. But you can judge that. As soon as I got a few feet into the cave, a fresh breeze hit my face. I thought there must be another opening somewhere ahead. I walked a little further into it, slowly, as it was quite dark, and I had no light. Suddenly, I felt as if the breeze were hitting under my chin, so I stopped, backed up a few feet, and got down on my hands and knees. I crawled very slowly forward, feeling my way, and then suddenly I could feel nothing under my hand as I put it forward. It was an eerie feeling, believe me. I fell flat on my stomach and dug my toes in for fear of falling over the edge of what appeared to be a chasm. I reached out to my side and found a large stone and dropped it ahead of me into the hole. I waited, and waited. But there was no sound of it hitting bottom, or anything. I waited for perhaps five minutes, and there wasn't a sound but the breeze hitting me, blowing up out of the hole. As far as I know, that stone never hit bottom. But I am going back to this cave soon, with plenty of rope and tools. I'll let you know what I find out—if I can find out anything at all. We'll see . . . Henry West, 138 Lincoln St., Midvale, Utah.

* * *

Which just about winds up this issue of the Club magazine. This first issue was quite a project, believe us! We were forced to reduce the number of pages we had originally scheduled because of increased typesetting prices, and paper shortages. But we'll be able to hold the club magazine at this size until things get a little better. Also, the letter section will get bigger as you interested people contribute your bit to help solve some of the things that go on in the world around us—unexplained. So let's all work together and prove or dis-prove anything that is said, thought about, or felt . . . Chester S. Geier.